ELVIS SPECIAL

A collection of photographs & features both fact & fictional written by Elvis' British fans and friends.

EDITED BY
ELVIS MONTHLY

World Distributors

A Member of the Pentos Group

ELVIS SPECIALWAS COMPILED FOR "ELVIS MONTHLY" BY TODD SLAUGHTER

We would like to thank all those writers who put so much into preparing their features for this edition of Elvis Special. As usual we thank those fans, fan clubs, film companies etc., for allowing us to use their photographs in this publication. We are indebted once again to Dutch cartoonist Ger Ryff for his drawings. Thanks are also extended to RCA, Colonel Parker, and to the late Elvis Presley, for making this publication possible.

THE WORLD

A TRIBUTE TO THE KING

Elvis Aaron Presley was born on January 8th 1935 in the two-roomed shack that was to be his home for many years to come. He was one of twins, the other one, Jesse, being born dead. His parents, Gladys and Vernon, never had another child so Elvis was brought up rather strictly. Neither of his parents were very well educated – they were slow at reading and writing, but morally they were very hard-working, God-fearing people.

From an early age it was apparent that Elvis loved singing; he and his parents would form a trio, Elvis and his father singing and Gladys playing the mouth organ, and they would play hymns and such at religious meetings.

When he was nine years old Elvis captivated his teacher at school, Mrs. J. C. Grimes, by saying a prayer and singing several songs in school assembly. One song in particular made Mrs. Grimes cry, that was *Old Shep*. He sang this same song some time later at an amateur singing contest at the Alabama-Mississippi Fair and won second prize, $5 and free admission to the sideshows.

For his birthday the following year his parents bought him a guitar; Elvis had wanted a bicycle but his parents knew they could never afford the $55. When his mother pointed out the guitar in the shop window to him he thought it a great idea, as already at that age he had ambitions to become a singer. Although he couldn't read music he learned chords from his two uncles, Vester Presley and Johnny Smith. He would listen to all the country performers on the radio, and by singing and playing at Church twice a week he was developing a love of spirituals and religious music.

In 1948 the family moved to Memphis. Vernon thought they would have the chance of a better future there, but at first things were no better. They lived in a single-room dwelling in a large house that had been converted into sixteen rooms such as they had. There was one bathroom to be shared between the tenants, and they had to cook on a hotplate in the same room as they lived, ate and slept. Vernon had a poorly paid job with a toolmaking firm and his mother also had to work. Elvis did sparetime jobs, mowing lawns and cleaning cars, anything to earn money to help the family. His mother's ill health forced her to give up her job so Elvis took an evening job as an usher at Loew's State Theater. He earned $14 a week, but his school work started to suffer because of the hours he worked. However, he was fired because another usher had told the manager that the girl selling sweets and popcorn had been giving some to Elvis – and Elvis had hit him. Still intent on helping out the family budget, Elvis got himself another night job, this time with the Marl Metal Products Company. But when he started dropping off to sleep at school his mother made him quit the job and *she* took another job at the local hospital.

Though he was now sixteen and approaching his last year at Humes High School, Elvis was still being strictly brought up by his parents. He thought the world of his mother and anything she asked him to do he would do. She didn't like him playing football in case he got hurt, she told him of the dangers of smoking and drinking . . . and he obeyed her in everything.

In only one thing did he rebel, and that was his appearance. Longing to be different, he grew his hair long and greased it heavily; he wore all black in order to stand out from the crowd and look older. He loved expensive clothes, but at that time could not afford to indulge in them. He would stand looking in the window of Lansky's Clothing Emporium on Beale Street, and often told Bernard Lansky he would one day buy him out. In 1953 Elvis graduated from Humes High School and took a job in a tool factory. Soon afterwards he applied for a job with the Crown Electric Company as a truck driver at $35 a week.

It was while he was driving his truck that he used to pass the Memphis Recording Service, where for a few dollars anyone could make a personal record. The service was used for recording weddings, and other personal events. Elvis thought it would be a good idea to sing a song for his mother's coming birthday.

Marion Keisker was the office Manager at the studio, which was a subsidiary of the Sun Record Company. When Elvis was halfway through his recording she realised that here was something different. She decided to tape the rest of the song

MOURNS ELVIS

My Happiness and let Sam Phillips, the owner, hear it.

Phillips came back from lunch while Elvis was still at the studio and he was impressed with the tape. He told Elvis he had promise, and took his name and work number in case he wanted to get in touch with him.

In 1953 the Presley family were dogged with ill health. Vernon was hospitalized for two weeks with a back complaint and when he returned home it became apparent that he would have to be off work for long periods. Elvis's mother's health also deteriorated – years of hard work and lack of good food were taking their toll of her.

Elvis began to realise that the only way he could help them would be to make the grade as a singer. In 1954 he returned to the Sun Studios to record *Casual Love* and *I'll Never Stand In Your Way*.

Marion Keisker and Sam Phillips were again both impressed by the singer, but at that time nothing came of it.

A few weeks later, however, Sam phoned Elvis at Crown Electric – he had a song he wanted to record and no singer available. He asked Elvis to do it for him. The record was not a success, but Phillips decided it was worth while persevering and he called in two musicians – Bill Black, bassist and Scotty Moore, guitarist – to work with Elvis.

They worked for some weeks on demonstration records for Phillips, but without a real hit. Then one night, after the three had been sitting chatting over a coffee break, Elvis suddenly sprang up with his guitar, and started singing *That's Alright Mama* – he was jumping around the studio and acting the fool, the other two joined him. Phillips suddenly appeared at the door and asked them what the hell they were doing.

"We don't know," said Scotty.

"Better find out fast," said Phillips, "and don't lose that sound."

They recorded the song, backed by *Blue Moon Of Kentucky* and Sam took the rough recording to Dewey Phillips, one of Memphis's top disc jockeys, and asked him to play it over the air.

Sam told Elvis the disc was to be played that night, but Elvis was overwhelmed and didn't dare to stay in and listen in case the record was a flop.

He went to see *High Noon* at the movies, leaving his parents to listen to the radio.

Halfway through the film his father came for him, telling him that Dewey Phillips wanted to see him at the radio station. He had played the record and had asked people for their opinion of it. Straight away he had had forty seven requests for it to be played again and fourteen telegrams asking when and where the record would be on sale.

Elvis arrived at the studio breathless to find out that Dewey wanted to interview him. He had been playing the record over and over and telling the listeners that he was hoping to get Elvis there for an interview before the show finished.

After the release of *That's Alright Mama* Elvis had his first big appearance at the Overton Park Shell Auditorium in Memphis. He had a small unbilled spot in the two performances. As Elvis sang, wriggled and shook on stage the audience went wild. Elvis was bewildered when he realised the effect he was having – but in an encore he shook and wriggled a lot more!

Elvis had signed a contract with Sun Records, but the firm wasn't able to pay a large advance of royalties on his records. So, briefly, Elvis had to return to his work at Crown Electric. When other jobs began to come in at local clubs, etc., he was able to leave his job at Crown. Then he was given spots on two top country radio shows, The Grand Ole Opry and Louisiana Hayride.

Colonel Parker first saw Presley in 1954, and after acquiring Elvis's management, and negotiating a switch from Sun to the US recording giant RCA, Elvis had his first worldwide smash with *Heartbreak Hotel* in 1956.

The rest is history. Live appearances, movies, television and record-breaking cabaret was to be the life style of Elvis Presley who, it is reported, has sold the equivalent of 800 million single-play records.

Elvis Presley died, aged 42, at his Memphis home around 2.30 pm on Tuesday, 16th August 1977. There is no finer tribute than to close by saying that the world will always remember Elvis – with love and devotion. Our sympathies are with the Presley family in Memphis.

Todd Slaughter

Softly, as I leave you …

Tracy is 15 years of age, lives in Southgate, and is a member of the North London branch of the fan club. A few months ago, she returned from the USA after seeing Elvis in concert at Philadelphia, thus fulfilling her father's death-bed wish.

In March of last year, her 55-year-old father, suffering from a brain tumour, was told by doctors at the University College Hospital in London that he had only three months to live. He kept this secret from both his wife and Tracy, and confided only in his best friend. It was only when he was admitted to the hospital that Tracy's mother found out, and then it was the doctors who told her. He was in the hospital for seven weeks, and for the last six days of his life, Mrs. Johnson did not leave his bedside. When the doctors told her they didn't think he would make it through another day, Tracy's aunt went and picked her up from school. Tracy went in to say goodbye to her father, and all she could do was kiss him and say, "I love you Daddy."

Tracy's Mum told me, "I will never forget those last minutes together, because when she had left the room, he turned to me and said he wanted me to send Tracy to America to see Elvis. It was something he had always wanted to do himself, because Tracy has always (since the age of five) been mad about Elvis, and used to say that he and her father were the most important men in her life. When he died, he left Tracy enough money to do just what he always wanted her to do. Ironically, he had planned to take us all to America for a holiday that summer."

Tracy's father died on the 25th May last year, just two weeks before Tracy's birthday.

When Tracy's mother contacted me with the news that Tracy was flying out to the States in the hope of seeing Elvis at home in Graceland, I found on checking her itinerary that she would be in Philadelphia on June 28th! Tracy was overjoyed, as it hadn't even entered her head that she might get to see a show, but just be lucky enough to see Elvis around Memphis. With the help of our friend and reporter Joe Tzouvanni, we managed to get Tracy's story front page coverage in the North London press.

Well, Tracy made it to the concert, and the story, in her own words, is here. Before she went, Tracy said, "I really do hope I can get to see Elvis, because somehow, knowing my father wanted me to makes it even more special." That Tracy deserved her moment of magic, there can be no doubt, and I feel sure that you are all as pleased for her as I am. I only hope that somehow her father knows that his wish came true.
Caroline Zetland

PHILADELPHIA SHOW of 28 June 1976—by Tracy
We arrived in Philadelphia on the 28th June, and through Caroline we knew that Elvis would be appearing there that very evening. We went to every ticket booth we could find, but naturally everywhere had sold out months before. But, if I couldn't see the actual show itself, I might stand a chance of seeing Elvis leaving the building. We caught the Subway to the "Spectrum" Stadium.

As I approached I could hear singing and various announcements. We then made our way to the main entrance, where there must have been at least 30 guards. We asked one of them if he knew which door Elvis would be leaving by, but he of course could not tell us. We then explained that we had come all the way from England, the object of our visit being to see Elvis. My heart sank slightly when I found out that there were at least 30–50 exits which Elvis could leave by. The guard offered us a ticket which someone had given him because they couldn't make it to the show themselves, but as I was a little nervous of going in alone with so many thousands of people, we thanked him for his offer but said that we would try to find two tickets together.

The King wasn't due on for another 30 minutes, and whilst we were waiting outside, yet another guard came up to us and said, "Did you want to go in?" (Ask a silly question, I thought to myself!) but said, "Yes, we'd like to," and explained how the other guard had offered me one ticket. He asked, "Would you like two seats together?" "If possible," was our immediate reply. We had previously noticed ticket touts selling tickets at prices that were beyond us, but the guard must have said something to them earlier, and one of them came up to us and GAVE us two seats next to each other! We couldn't believe our luck!

When we reached our seats, we had a lovely view of the stage, and the "Sweet Inspirations" were on. Then came the break, during which there were notices one after the other about Elvis items on sale in the Stadium. After the 15 minute interval, the houselights went off, the stage lights went on, and Elvis' group played his theme tune, 2001, then yet another spot-light came up and Elvis appeared. He was clad in white trousers with decoration up the sides of them, a thick white belt studded with a gold-coloured metal, and a pale blue shirt.

There's no need to really say what happened next; from the girls there came screams of "Elvis, I love you," and even the men were calling and clapping for him. Then, he started singing! He only had to sing the first couple of words before everyone started cheering.

By now, girls were pushing their way to the front of the stage, holding their hands out to him. He then kneeled down and kissed some of them. After he finished that song, he said, "Good evening" and thanked everyone for coming. He then started singing the word "well" in different keys, and then said, "Well, thanks for having me folks, I've got to go now!" Everybody laughed and he even gave a little chuckle. He then chatted to the audience for about five minutes and then broke into a sentimental song, and all the girls started crying for him. He kissed several of them, and held the microphone near one girl and as he did, she said, "Elvis, I love you."

After he finished, he threw the guitar that he was carrying through the air to Charlie, and later on during the evening, he took off the scarf he was wearing and threw into the audience. He had at least two dozen of these, which he either put around his neck for a few minutes and then threw, or he wiped the sweat from his brow and then threw. When Elvis sang the song which I believe is "the Elvis song", what else but *Jailhouse Rock*? he really did live up to the name of "the man with the swivelling hips". As he swivelled those gorgeous hips, all the girls gave a deafening scream, and Elvis gave a deliberate look down to his trousers as if he expected them to be split! The look of horror disappeared when he saw that he was still in one piece, and he carried on singing.

Where the newspapers get the idea that he's overweight, I don't know, as when I saw him at the Spectrum, he wasn't the slightest bit overweight. He was just beautiful, and very tall and broad-shouldered.

Near the front of the stage sat a girl holding a toy pink panther for Elvis to take, which he did. He stood in the centre of the stage for a couple of seconds, wearing a battered hat which someone had given him, pulled practically over his eyes.

By now, the guards had started lining up in front of the stage, and as the girls kept pushing their way towards the front, Elvis kept saying, "Be careful honey."

As I have mentioned earlier, the Spectrum is a massive place, and when Elvis sang the first few

words of *America the Beautiful* everybody stood up, all the 10–15 thousand that were there, and sang along with him.

After everyone was seated, he said, "Would you like to hear my new song?" and the building was filled with cries of "Yes!" Never in my life have I heard a song sung as he sang *Hurt*. He held the microphone at least a foot away from his mouth, but he sang so strongly that the room vibrated. When he finished, everybody loved it so much, he said, "Would you like to hear it again?" and needless to say, the answer was "Yes!" How he managed to improve on the song the second time around, is beyond belief, because it was too wonderful the first time to be even the slightest bit improved upon, but being Elvis, he managed the impossible. The live version far surpasses the recorded one. What a pity RCA weren't taping this show!

He then thanked us for having him, and said, "You just let me know when you want us back again."

Naturally, these weren't the only things that happened, but I was so overwhelmed with his performance, that I can't remember every single detail.

Tracy then visited Graceland, and had a nice friendly chat with Uncle Vester in the gate house. He then took her on a tour of the grounds in the jeep, gave her a photo of Elvis, and a kiss on the cheek!

Unfortunately, Elvis was with Lisa in Los Angeles at the time Tracy was in Memphis. A couple of the

interesting little episodes regarding Elvis that were related to Tracy whilst she was at Graceland she has passed on to us, and we hope you enjoy reading them.

Apparently, one night in Dallas, Elvis had left the stage, and was running—surrounded as usual by bodyguards—towards the exit where his three limousines were waiting. However, instead of making straight for the car, Elvis had to make a quick detour to visit the bathroom. Unfortunately, none of the bodyguards realised that he had gone, and all proceeded to pile into the waiting cars, the occupants of each car assuming that Elvis was in one of the others. The cars then shot off in the direction of the airport, leaving Elvis alone in the corridor behind the stage!

When the cars reached the airport and all the passengers got out, they were suddenly hit with the realisation that somebody was missing!!! There is no need to tell the speed with which those cars retraced their journey back to the stadium! Meanwhile Elvis, finding himself literally deserted became—to say the least—rather alarmed, which is natural when there are about 10,000 people screaming and running around the area, "trying to get to you"! In panic, he hid behind a trash-can so as not to be seen, and that is where his people found him when they arrived back at the venue! Hardly a fitting place for a King! (I bet a few heads rolled that night!)

One evening, a party of around 200 fans were gathered at the gates of Graceland, when Elvis and one of his side-kicks appeared, racing their go-karts around the grounds. By the time the fans realised who was in the karts, Elvis had shot round and gone out of the back gate. The fans thought the person driving round the grounds was still Elvis, and were all calling to him.

Meantime, Elvis had gone out of the back gate, stopped the go-kart, and was standing on it, looking over the wall, leaning on his hands and calling out, "Ppssssttt! I'm over here!"

When the guards told the fans where Elvis was, nobody took any notice, all being quite convinced that the man driving around the grounds was he. All the time Elvis was still calling out, "Ppsssstt! I'm over here!" and at last someone realised where he was.

At this point, everyone who had previously been at the front gate, started running down the side passage to get to Elvis, and all that could be seen from the front of the grounds was a cloud of dust coming over the wall from the running feet!

At this juncture Elvis made a quick retreat into the side gate, and the guards closed it pretty quickly! Elvis proceeded to tease everyone outside, by putting his head over the gate, quivering his lip, and shaking his legs!

THE ELVIS PRESLEY DORSEY SHOWS

An early account of Elvis' Television Appearances
written by PAUL DOWLING

Ask anyone what Elvis Presley's first television appearance was and, more than likely, the answer would be the *Ed Sullivan Shows*, (September, October 1956 and January 1957). Question them further and they might come up with *Steve Allen* (1 July 1956). If you're lucky the next guess would be *Milton Berle* (3 April and 5 June 1956). But the answer would still be wrong! Actually, Elvis first appeared on TV on 28 January 1956 on the *Tommy and Jimmy Dorsey Stage Show*, a 30-minute programme on CBS, and he performed on their show five more times after this, making his last appearance in late March.

Before going any further into discussing each show, it would be appropriate to clear up a few misconceptions about them. Many believe that Elvis was on a few *Jackie Gleason Shows* in early 1956, but, upon careful checking, no information can be found. This is because the STAGE SHOWS were Jackie Gleason produced programmes and were shown either prior or following *Gleason's Honeymooners* series. The 28 January, 4 February and 11 February Dorsey shows were aired "live" at 8 pm (New York time) followed by the *Honeymooners*. Then, on 18 February the two shows were reversed with Gleason's half-hour starting off and the "live" Dorsey half-hour next. This continued at least until the last Elvis performance on 24 March. Each Dorsey programme usually consisted of two other acts besides Elvis, most of the guests being well-known celebrities like Sarah Vaughan, Joe E. Brown, Ella Fitzgerald or up and coming stars like Gene Sheldon and Henny Youngman. Apparently, no other rock 'n' roll artists ever appeared before or after Elvis did in the history of the Dorsey shows, which must say something about this new type of music that was to change the industry only a few months later.

Elvis' first song to the American public on 28 January was *Blue Suede Shoes* which he hadn't even recorded yet. (NOTE: this was recorded two days later at the RCA studios in New York). This was done very similar to the version on the first LP (LPM 1254). "Thank you ladies and gentlemen, and now a little song I have on record—RCA Victor—called *Heartbreak Hotel* . . ." Hotel had been recorded on 10 January and had just been released although it wasn't until this show that the song started to take off. The Dorsey band backed Elvis on this number and, half way through, they couldn't keep up with his beat, thus making the end result very awkward sounding. Why the Dorseys decided to back him anyway is certainly a puzzle, but it was the first and last time they did! Elvis moved quite a bit during *Blue Suede Shoes* but the audience merely applauded more as a kind gesture than anything else, and, at times, seemed quite confused at what was happening.

Reaction to his leg movements increased the following week (4 February) and his initial number, *Tutti Frutti*, brought clapping from the audience as he began his act during the instrumental break. *I Was the One* followed and was done almost the same as on the recorded version. It is not known if the Jordanaires were backing Elvis this early but there were *some* backing vocals on this number. The second show brought more response from the audience than the first and the Hillbilly Cat was beginning to catch on.

Cleveland, Ohio disc jockey Bill Randall (who was then doing a weekend show in New York) introduced Elvis on the third show (11 February). "We'd like at this time to introduce you to a young fellow who, like many performers—Johnny Ray among them—came up out of nowhere to become big stars. This young fellow we saw for the first time while making a movie short and we think tonight he's going to make television history for you. We'd like you to meet him tonight—Elvis Presley."

Elvis tore into *Shake, Rattle and Roll* and sang a real rockin' version which nearly drove the audience wild as he changed the final verse to ". . . I'm like a Mississippi bullfrog sitting on a hollow stump. I got so many women I don't know which way to jump!" He also went into the song *Flip, Flop and Fly* and used this for the ending much as he did nearly 20 years later during the concerts in the early 1970s. *I Got a Woman* closed his portion of the show and Elvis did this like his recorded version. It must be noted that this was the first show that produced screams from girls in the audience as compared to the clapping on the first two programmes.

By the fourth show (18 February), Presleymania had spread and Elvis was the biggest new name in the music business in years. The Dorsey shows began clobbering competition in the ratings and a new type of singer and music had been born. Never had the public seen a man shake his legs in spasmodic contortions but, even more dramatic, the suggestive words that Elvis was singing caused an uproar among sponsors, parents, and in fact the entire American people. The third show started it with, "I got so many women I don't know which way to jump," but the fourth heightened it with his repeated ". . . come back baby, I wanna play house with you!" This was just not the thing to say on nationwide television in 1956 but it was "live" so it couldn't be stopped. Elvis was inviting girls openly on TV to live with him! *Baby Let's Play House* on this show must rank as one of his wildest and best performances on TV as he not only sang a much sexier version than his SUN recording, but he moved with apparent sexual abandon during the instrumental breaks, uttering phrases like "go wild!!!" before attacking his guitar strings and moving all over the stage. Bill Black watched, bewildered, as Elvis gave the performance of his then two-year lifetime! This was followed by another rocker . . . "and now a little song that tells a story, really makes a lot of sense,"—*Tutti Frutti*, which was even wilder than on the second show and Elvis went all out to please his ever-growing fan following.

Elvis *did not* appear on the 25 February, 3 March or 10 March STAGE SHOWS as he was probably doing the Louisiana Hayride shows on these Saturdays. His fifth appearance was 7 March and he began with *Blue Suede Shoes*. From the opening, "Well, it's a one for the money . . ." the audience started screaming and didn't let up until his second song was over. "Thank you very much, that was my latest RCA Victor escape, uh release. We have another song here friends which we hope you like. It's called *Heartbreak Hotel*. . . ." This was the second time Elvis had sung *Heartbreak Hotel* on the Dorsey shows and, by this time, the song was either number one or close to it.

The sixth and final show was on 24 March. Elvis came out wearing a dark brown suit, dark shirt, and white tie (with a large knot). His then blondish hair shook as he went through his wild gyrations during the instrumental break of the first song, *Money Honey*, doing it much better than the take on his first LP. The final song was *Heartbreak Hotel* and Elvis moved even more, twisting and holding his left leg, thrusting it out in every direction possible! His legs seemed to have a mind of their own! There was no doubt that a new American hero had arrived!

On all the Dorsey programmes Elvis moved chiefly during the instrumental breaks as Scotty Moore, Bill Black, and D. J. Fontana provided the backing beat. It was not impossible for him to go through his stage antics while singing, but, since the microphone

on all six shows was stationary, it was best for him to do so mainly during the breaks. The type of motions he performed on these shows was entirely different from any on subsequent TV shows like *Ed Sullivan* and, as he hadn't yet been restricted from performing like he was used to, he apparently let loose with all he had. Also, Elvis played his guitar like crazy, using it as an instrument rather than as a prop, which it was basically used for later on in his career.

One must give Jackie Gleason a lot of the credit for making Elvis Presley into the household name he is today. To take a performer as different as Elvis was then and to showcase him on a nationwide television show took a lot of nerve in 1956. This was Elvis' big break and he took full advantage of it. These early TV appearances, even though they are practically unknown by most Elvis fans and even forgotten by others, were the backbone of the Elvis Presley saga and were the beginnings of the legend of the greatest rock 'n' roll singer and performer of all time!

THE BIG ONE

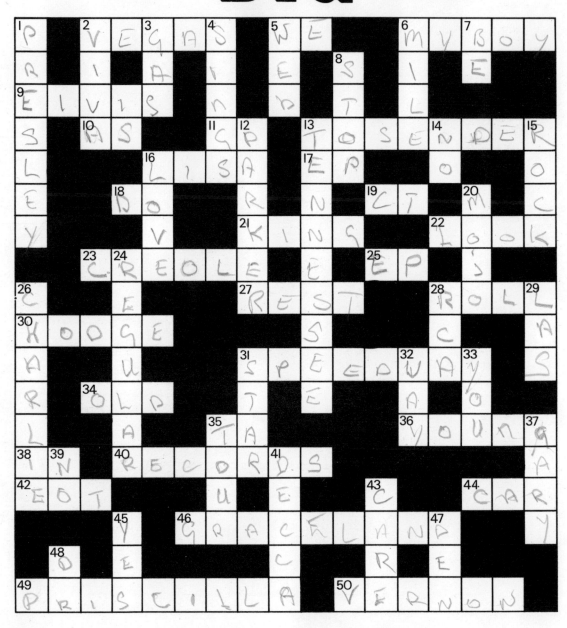

ACROSS

2 Belongs to 29 Down—end of our pilgrimage.
5 All of us.
6 1975 hit (early) or late 1974, whichever's the easiest.
9 A name we all love.
10 *Softly — I Leave You.*
11 Elvis was one in 1969 (film abbrev).
13 Song mentioning return.
16 He has idolised this person since 1968.
17 His initials.
18 The clam.
19 Manager's initials (first two).
21 Elvis is — of 15 Down and 28 Across.
22 *Stop — Listen.*
23 Another royal name.
25 Not a 45 or LP, an in between.
27 Elvis has earned a long —.
28 End of his title.
30 Other half of 26 Down.
31 Film portraying a racing car driver.
34 Song about dog called Shep.
35 When 16 Across was small, Elvis would say — instead of please or thank you.
36 Elvis once described someone as — and beautiful (from *Worldwide 25 Gold Award Hits Vol. 3*).

12

38 He isn't out.
40 These are very popular with fans.
42 Last film made (initials only).
44 He has many of these, this is just one.
46 One of his many residences.
49 Elvis is still very close with this person.
50 One of two who made Elvis possible.

DOWN

1 A well loved surname.
2 Combine 2 Across and 29 Down, and you also get a film.
3 Elvis puts this in 44 Across.
4 When Elvis — we all applaude.
5 How the — was woven.
6 Walk a — in Elvis' shoes.
7 *How Would You Like to —*.
8 *— Look and Listen*.
12 Surname of 19 Across.
13 To see 46 Across you need to be in the right State.
14 Ask the Colonel to get Elvis to England, and the answer would be —.

15 First part of his title—also a well-known gift from seaside.
16 We are asked to do this to him tenderly.
20 Has he got his — working.
24 Make sure you have a — order of E/M.
26 One of his close friends who looks after him on stage.
28 Record label (abbrev).
29 Put this with 2 Down and 2 Across, you have a place and film.
31 He certainly is a big one.
32 What we ask when Elvis isn't coming to England.
33 Not me, I or we but —.
35 Elvis does this when not appearing in Las Vegas.
37 A famous pepper.
39 The answer is still — from the Colonel.
41 His closest friend in show business had/has a contract with this Record Company.
43 — About Elvis the rest will follow later E/M 182.
45 If we all talked to Elvis maybe his answer would be —.
47 Elvis may have one in his home (a place for his hobbies and games etc) —.
48 11 Across could also be abbrev to —.

Answers on page 62

ELVIS WANTS YOU TO JOIN HIS FAN CLUB

It's now time for you to show your support and join the "World's most respected" fan club—the OFFICIAL ELVIS PRESLEY FAN CLUB OF GREAT BRITAIN AND THE COMMONWEALTH. When you become a member you automatically become part of the greatest fan-friendship organisation in existence, and although our club is the largest of its kind any-where, personal attention for you is our prime objective. Upon joining you will receive a membership pass and the fan club magazine—packed with news and pictures about Elvis Presley, the fan club, its activities, special offers, and members' services. And during the year you'll receive a further five magazines despatched to you at regular two-monthly intervals.

FAN CLUB SERVICES: Throughout the year you'll be informed of fan club special offers, such as pens, stationery, tee shirts, badges, posters, and photographs. We operate a comprehensive branch leader network, and it is most likely you already have a club branch secretary serving your area, who will organise regular get-togethers, parties and coach outings to fan club events and film shows. Branch leader listings are published regularly in the fan club magazine. Want a pen-pal, or do you want to swop Elvis items with another fan? It's all done through the club magazine.

FAN CLUB HOLIDAYS: Over the past six years the fan club has taken members overseas on special cut-price holidays and long weekends. Trips have been organised to Belgium, Luxembourg, Holland, Germany and France, and DESTINATION USA—an exclusive charter holiday for Elvis fan club members—visits Nashville, Memphis, Tupelo, Las Vegas, Hollywood, Los Angeles, and Mexico during a two week period each year when we are able to see Elvis live in concert in Las Vegas, as well as visiting some of the places where Elvis has been during his career. USA '78 is currently being planned, but you have to be a member to come along with us.

FAN CLUB EVENTS: Nearer to home, throughout the year the club organises film shows all over the UK in major cities, and each year there's the FAN CLUB CONVENTION. Attracting over 2,000 fans this special show is organised in aid of the Guide Dogs for the Blind Association. As well as the very best films and on-stage entertainment, you'll be greeted by special surprise guests. Some who have attended in the past include Alvin Stardust, Jimmy Savile, Tony Prince, Rosko, Kid Jensen, Anita Harris, Paul Burnett, Spencer Davis, Dave Christian, and Johnny Moran, and our shows have been recorded for Radio Luxembourg, BBC1 TV, ITV, French, German and Dutch TV, as well as MGM pictures. Our Convention in Luxembourg was part of the MGM movie *Elvis— That's the Way it is.*

For further details send a stamped addressed envelope to: ELVIS PRESLEY FAN CLUB, PO BOX 4, LEICESTER.

TODD SLAUGHTER

AN OPEN LETTER TO ELVIS

It's Midnight, and I miss you. With the words of the song still ringing in my ears, I stare at a newspaper cutting that bears the awful headlines "ELVIS THINKS FANS DONT CARE"—and it hurts me, it hurts me so bad I can't sleep. I cannot believe that you could think this Elvis, because we do care, I care. . . .

I care very much. I care about you enough that I made the trip to America in 1973 to see you and you alone, I spent money I could hardly afford to give myself the thrill of seeing you, I spent money to get close to you, hundreds of dollars just for a ring-side seat, and that first year I was rewarded, I got a blue scarf. . . .

I care, oh I care, I cared enough dear Elvis to save again for a second year in 1974, to come to Vegas once more to be thrilled by your voice. I was doubly rewarded this time, I got four scarves and two kisses. Elvis you think we don't care, when fans such as I care too much, care about you so bad that I risk my home and family just to be near you, just to feel your presence in a room full of people. Elvis the ones who really care for you and love you are pushed out in the cold, oh, not by you, you radiate love from that stage Elvis, you make each fan who crosses your path feel wanted and loved—but Elvis we cannot get near you any other way.

I appreciate the fact you were ill in 1974 and were meeting no one or very few, but Elvis if you are afraid no one cares, then listen here, those who really love you and care for you wanted to meet you, only the false hangers-on ever seem to get to you, those who use you and want to boast they have met Elvis Presley. The ones who really love you, who cherish your very name, who want to meet you for yourself, are thrown aside, and yet we still love you, we care even more because we realise the pressures put upon you. . . .

The newspaper article says that those who could cure you are locked out, true, so true, meaning us the devoted fans, you are afraid we don't care . . . if we could meet you, talk with you, then you would see just how much we care. . . .

Elvis you don't see the things you should see, people hide you away from reality so much you miss out on the true emotions of your fans. If you could see a few of the things that happen then you would know how much we care.

When I first saw Memphis in 1973 Elvis, I viewed it from the tenth floor of a hotel. I first saw the lights of Memphis at 4.00 am, it started to rain, and I started to cry, and I kept on crying, because I was there, the place I cared about, your home town. I cried at your mother's grave, because I cared that she brought you into the world, she gave me someone to love—you. I cried when I saw you on stage, you know I even cried when you did your Karate in 1974. Why? Because I care, you get to my very soul Elvis.

It breaks my heart to read such headlines Elvis, how true paper talk is who can say? I know you feel most magazines are junk, I agree oh I agree, but this hits hard, these cold black headlines. How does a person get through to you Elvis, how does a fan tell you she cares? Who wants to listen? But I think you should listen Elvis, I think you should read this, how can I prove to you how I and so many others feel? Frustration at this point is a gross understatement Elvis, not being able to reach you with these words of caring. . . .

You're ill Elvis, the minute I hear it I send you a get well card, I send you other cards and letters, I do everything except fly out to you, but if I did, who would let me near you? No-one, so how can you know how one cares? You're the King, a superstar, you're unique—but you're also a human being Elvis, wouldn't you like just once to sit and talk with a fan? A fan who does care? Not to talk about showbusiness, but anything you choose, we are not empty-headed people, we are not children, you are a man, a very intelligent man who can converse on something more than mere Teddy Bears and Hound Dogs, that I know. I witnessed your intellect, Elvis, in Vegas, you're the most interesting man I have ever set eyes upon. . . .

Oh yes Elvis someone cares, but as long as the doors are kept locked, you, my number one man, will never know. If this letter is published I doubt if you'll ever see it, but I just wish with all my heart that someone would show you this, let you read it, and maybe someone will think hard about those such as I who have spent their lives being devoted to you. I am locked out completely this year, because I cannot afford the trip to dreamsville to be with you, but no matter how far I am away from you I care . . . oh yes, it's midnight and I miss you.

Elvis, I will spend my whole life through—Loving You.

PAT BARRS

ELVIS IN THE MOVIES

LOVE ME TENDER (20th Century Fox) 1956
Vance—Richard Egan
Cathy—Debra Paget
Clint—Elvis Presley

Producer—David Weisbart
Director—Robert D. Webb

For a first attempt, and with co-star billing, Elvis tackled an interesting story, but a tame script. Yet for Elvis fans *Love Me Tender* was his first movie, and a chance for overseas fans to catch a glimpse of Elvis walking, talking, singing, and crying. We sat anxiously awaiting the first sighting of the master, and there in a distant field, pulling a plough (America had yet to discover oil, and invent the petrol engine) was the super-giant of pop. It was the end of the civil war. Elvis' brother was a Confederate, and with his troop, had pillaged a Federal payroll, thinking that the war was still in full swing. Soon after they learned that the war was over, and instead of returning the booty to the authorities, they decided to split the spoils. Elvis had by now married his brother's fiancée, assuming that he had died in battle, and when the missing son returned home problems began. The old love is rekindled, and the authorities turn up to reclaim the stolen money.

A double-double-cross takes place, and Elvis is shot dead. The first and only time Elvis actually dies in front of a cinema audience (though it's assumed in *Flaming Star*), and as the title song is played during the scene, a valley of tears sweeps across the paying customers.

LOVING YOU (Paramount) 1957

Deke Rivers—Elvis Presley
Glenda Markle—Lizabeth Scott
Walter "Tex" Warner—Wendell Corey
Carl—James Gleason

Producer—Hal Wallis
Director—Hal Kanter

Young Deke Rivers is seen singing with an unsuccessful band by the ex-wife of the Band leader. She recognises Deke's talent and the effect he has on the audience and realises that he could help her ex-husband back to popularity. Glenda makes him believe she has fallen in love with him in her efforts to raise him to popularity by causing hysteria amongst the teenage fans. Deke is bewildered by his sudden rise to fame. He learns of her deceit just before an important TV spectacular and drives off, but of course is brought back for the show which inevitably brings him fame and stardom.

JAILHOUSE ROCK (M.G.M.) 1957

Vince Everett—Elvis Presley
Peggy Van Alden—Judy Tyler
Hunk Houghton—Mickey Shaughnessy
Sherry Wilson—Jennifer Holden
Teddy Talbot—Dean Jones

Producer—Pandro S. Berman
Director—Richard Thorpe

Vince Everett and Hunk Houghton meet in jail after Vince is imprisoned for manslaughter after an accidental killing. Hunk sees that Vince has musical talents and they agree to form a partnership when they are released. Vince however is the first to be released and is discovered by Peggy Van Alden, a talent scout. Vince becomes a big star before Hunk is released from prison, and his head is turned by his rise to fame. A fight ensues between the two former friends and Vince sustains an injury to his throat which threatens his career. He is nursed back to health by Peggy, who loves him, and Hunk, who has remained his friend throughout.

KING CREOLE (Paramount) 1958

Danny Fisher—Elvis Presley
Ronnie—Carolyn Jones
Nellie—Dolores Hart
Mr. Fisher—Dean Jagger
Maxie Fields—Walter Matthau
Based on "A Stone for Danny Fisher" by Harold Robbins

Producer—Hal Wallis
Director—Michael Curtiz

This is considered to be Elvis' own favourite film. In it he plays Danny Fisher, whose father is pressing him to do well and to earn a living. Thinking it will be easy money, he takes part in a shoplifting raid which is successful. Nellie (played by Dolores Hart) does her best to persuade him to give up the life of crime. This is not so easy for Danny as the night club he works at is run by a vicious gangster. After Danny is signed by a rival night club, the "King Creole" loses customers and Maxie orders one of his henchmen to involve Danny in a crime in an effort to win him back. There is an attack on Danny's father's employer and Mr. Fisher gets beaten up.

Maxie Fields pays the hospital bills for looking after Mr. Fisher so Danny is again in his clutches, and has to work in his club again. Maxie tells Mr. Fisher that it is Danny who beat him up with the result that Danny has a showdown with Fields. All's well that ends well when Danny is reconciled with his father and Nellie again.

G.I. BLUES (Paramount) 1960

Tulsa McLean—Elvis Presley	Producer—Hal Wallis
Lilli—Juliet Prowse	Director—Norman Taurog
Cooky—Robert Ivers	
Tina—Leticia Roman	

Elvis plays the part of Tulsa McLean, a G.I. who, together with two other G.I.s plays in a group and has ambitions to open a night club when they are demobbed. Lilli is a popular dancer who is reputed to be an iceberg, and Tulsa makes a bet with his buddies that he will spend a night with her.

He meets Lilli and, with the others watching his every move, charms her. They eventually do spend a night together but only baby sitting. However Tulsa has won his bet and the money is his. When Lilli finds out about the gamble she thinks Tulsa wanted only to win the bet and does not care about her. However, everything is sorted out satisfactorily in the end and love triumphs.

FOLLOW THAT DREAM (United Artists) 1962

Toby Kwimper—Elvis Presley	Producer—David Weisbart
Pop Kwimper—Arther O'Connell	Director—Gordon Douglas
Holly Jones—Anne Helm	
Alicia Claypoole—Joanna Moore	

One of Elvis' funniest films and one which ought to have won him an Oscar in the opinion of many people. *Follow That Dream* is the story of Pop Kwimper, his son Toby and a family of four orphans. This homeless crowd stop on the highway and when the authorities try to move them on Pop decides to homestead on a strip of beach alongside the highway. It is not long before more trailers join them and a small community is established. However, a gambler also arrives on the scene and opens up a gambling den which soon gives the place a bad name. The rest of the small community elect Toby as sheriff and his first duty is to notify the gambler that he is breaking the law. The gangster orders his hoods to get rid of Toby but through a lot of luck and some misunderstandings Toby gets the better of them.

The orphans are taken by the State and Pop has to attend a hearing in court, but Toby's courage and tenacity so impress the judge that they are all able to stay together.

BLUE HAWAII (Paramount) 1961

Chad Gates—Elvis Presley	Producer—Hal Wallis
Maile Duval—Joan Blackman	Director—Norman Taurog
Sarah Lee Gates—Angela Lansbury	
Abigail Prentace—Nancy Walters	

After a series of misunderstandings with his parents (who also disapprove of his girlfriend Maile) Chad Gates takes a job as a tourist guide to a schoolteacher and her four charges (all female). After even more misunderstandings between Chad, his girlfriend, the four schoolgirls, as well as his mother—he eventually manages to sort the situation out for a satisfactory conclusion.

This film has sometimes been quoted as Elvis' most successful film, but being rather a mild plot much of the success must be due to the scenery and "Elvis".

WILD IN THE COUNTRY (20th Century Fox)

Glenn—Elvis Presley	Producer—Jerry Wald
Irene—Hope Lange	Director—Philip Dunne
Noreen—Tuesday Weld	
Betty Lee—Millie Perkins	
Phil Macy—John Ireland	

Glenn is a young man who wants to write. He undeservedly gets a reputation for violence with the result that he is ordered to see a psychiatrist. This is Irene Sperry and she and his girlfriend encourage him in his writing ambitions. Glenn has made enemies in the past however, one his Uncle Rolfe and another one, Cliff, the son of wealthy lawyer Phil Macy, who wants to marry Irene. After many complications, in which Cliff spreads rumours about his relationship with Irene, Glenn and Cliff have a fight in which Cliff (who unknown to Glenn has a weak heart) dies. Glenn is arrested and because Cliff's father witholds evidence about his son's heart condition, it seems likely that Glenn will be found guilty of the killing. An attempted suicide by Irene brings everyone to their senses however and Glenn is free to go to college and pursue his writing.

FLAMING STAR (20th Century Fox) 1960

Pacer—Elvis Presley
Roslyn Pierce—Barbara Eden
Clint—Steve Forrest
Neddy Burton—Dolores Del Rio
Pa Burton—John McIntire

Producer—David Weisbart
Director—Don Siegel

Pacer is the half-breed son of a white father and Indian mother. The trouble starts after the massacre of a family when Pacer is accused by the townspeople of helping in the raid. When his father refuses to join in a reprisal raid, Pacer's brother Clint shoots one of the members who insults his mother. The Indians think Pacer should join them and his mother is seriously injured whilst trying to make peace between them.

The townspeople will not allow them any medical help until in desperation Pacer and his brother hold a child hostage. His mother dies before a doctor can arrive and Pacer is turned against whites. Brother hates brother until their father is injured, then Pacer is mortally wounded, and they all meet up for their final reunion.

KID GALAHAD (United Artists) 1962

Walter Gulick—Elvis Presley
Willy Grogan—Gig Young
Dolly Fletcher—Lola Albright
Rose Grogan—Joan Blackman
Lew Nyack—Charles Bronson

Producer—David Weisbart
Director—Phil Karlson

Walter Gulick, just out of the Army and broke, takes a job as a sparring partner at a training camp for fighters. His opponent is well known for slaughtering his sparring partners, but with a bit of luck Walter knocks him out. When someone makes a pass at Dolly, Willy Grogan's girlfriend, Walter throws the man out through the door, and Dolly nicknames Walter "Kid Galahad". Walter fights under this name and becomes well known for his quick knock-outs. Walter meets Rose, Willy's sister, and they fall in love. He wants to get out of the fighting business and settle down with her but he has one big fight to get through first.

Despite efforts to bribe him to throw the fight, and a savage brawl, Walter wins through and the film ends with Walter and Rose in each other's arms and a rosy future ahead of them.

GIRLS! GIRLS! GIRLS! (Paramount) 1962

Ross Carpenter—Elvis Presley
Robin Gantner—Stella Stevens
Laurel Dodge—Laurel Goodwin
Wesley Johnson—Jeremy Slate

Producer—Hal Wallis
Director—Norman Taurog

Acclaimed as one of the Elvis Film Classics this film with its bevy of beautiful girls and good songs was bound to be a hit.

Ross Carpenter is skipper of a charter fishing boat belonging to Alexander Stavros, who also owns the "West Wind", a sailboat built by Ross and his father before the latter's death. This boat is the love of Ross's life, but unfortunately due to a financial crisis Stavros has to sell it to a hard businessman, Wesley Johnson, who doubles the boat's price. Ross sees his ambition of ever earning enough money to buy the boat failing. Meanwhile he falls in love with Laurel Dodge, who unknown to Ross is the daughter of a wealthy man. With money from her father she buys the "West Wind" as a gift for Ross, but when he finds out he is furious as he sees the gift as charity. After an angry scene he walks off and leaves her utterly miserable. Laurel sets out after Ross in the boat with Wesley Johnson and Ross, seeing them together, mistakes Johnson's intentions, boards the boat and attacks him. However, later at a colourful party all misunderstandings are cleared and Ross and Laurel are reunited when Ross proposes marriage to a very happy girl.

IT HAPPENED AT THE WORLDS FAIR (M.G.M.) 1963

Mike Edwards—Elvis Presley
Diane Warren—Joan O'Brien
Danny Burke—Gary Lockwood

Producer—Ted Richmond
Director—Norman Taurog

Mike and Danny are two bush pilots, Mike with a weakness for girls, Danny with a weakness for gambling, with the result that they are usually found to be permanently broke. Their latest escapades have made them penniless, job-less and their plane has been taken as security for all the bills they owe.

Whilst looking for work they meet a Chinese farmer taking his little niece Sue-Lin to the Worlds Fair in Seattle. When Uncle Walter has to do some unexpected business it becomes impossible for him to take the little girl to the fair so Mike offers to take her instead. While Danny searches for an old friend to help them out of their financial troubles Mike and Sue-Lin enjoy all the rides at the fair. After eating a variety of "goodies" Sue-Lin gets stomach ache and Mike takes her for medical attention and meets a pretty nurse, Diane, on whom Mike's charms have little effect. Later they find Uncle Walter is missing and Sue-Lin is taken to the Welfare Board.

Meanwhile Danny has found his shady friend who has put forward the money they need to get their plane back in exchange for them flying a cargo to Canada for him. Just before take-off Mike finds out that Sue-Lin has escaped from the Welfare Board and he finds her at the fair.

In the chaos that follows the two friends find out that their cargo is contraband furs. Eventually all is sorted out to the good of Mike and Danny and Uncle Walter is found in hospital, only slightly injured after an accident. Together Mike and Diane visit the fair, happy in their new found love, and together they enlist in the US Aerospace Programme.

FUN IN ACAPULCO (Paramount) 1963

Mike Windgren—Elvis Presley
Margareta Dauphine—Ursula Andress
Dolores Gomez—Elsa Cardenas
Maximillian—Paul Lukas

Producer—Hal Wallis
Director—Richard Thorpe

Mike Windgren goes to Acapulco to forget a trapeze accident in the States when he accidentally let his partner fall and badly injured him. Mike has a fear of heights as the result of this accident and has to find himself a different job. Whilst singing by night in an hotel and being a lifeguard by day at the same hotel he meets and becomes attracted to the hotel's social director, Margareta Dauphine.

Moreno, another lifeguard, is jealous of Mike's attention to Margareta and when he finds out about Mike's fear of heights he thinks of a way of proving himself superior to Mike in Margareta's eyes. Moreno does a spectacular dive off the cliffs every night into the sea and he has an argument with Mike which ends with them fighting.

The outcome of this is that Moreno pretends to be too injured to make the dive, so Mike decides to conquer his fear and make the dive in his place. Mike's dive is successful, and he emerges from the water triumphant and wins the girl.

VIVA LAS VEGAS (M.G.M.) 1964

(Retitled UK—Love in Las Vegas)

Lucky Jackson—Elvis Presley
Rusty Martin—Ann-Margaret
Count Mancini—Cesare Donova
Mr. Martin—William Demarest

Producers Jack Cummings/George Sidney
Director—George Sidney

Lucky Jackson has an ambition to be the World's racing champion. He arrives in Las Vegas for a Grand Prix and meets Count Mancini, the Italian racing champion, who is intent on winning the race by whatever means he can. Lucky falls for Rusty Martin when she asks him and Mancini to fix her sports car. She is the swimming instructress at the hotel where Lucky is staying. After falling in the swimming pool and losing the money intended for a new engine, Lucky enters a talent competition but finds on winning it that no cash is involved, only a gold cup and a honeymoon ticket to Las Vegas.

When it looks as if Lucky's chances of even starting in the race are dwindling, the money for the engine turns up (a secret gift from Rusty's rich father). He makes the starting line just in time and a fast and furious race ensues. Lucky, of course, wins and marries the girl as well.

KISSIN' COUSINS (M.G.M.) 1964

Josh Morgan ⎫ Elvis Presley
Jodie Tatum ⎭
Pappy Tatum—Arthur O'Connell
Ma Tatum—Glena Farrell
Capt. Robert Salbo—Jack Albertson

Producer—Sam Katzman
Director—Gene Nelson

In this film Elvis plays a dual role which is a treat for all Elvis fans. Jodie Tatum lives with his father and family on Big Smokey Mountain in Tennessee which Pa Tatum owns. The US Air Force wants to build a missile base on top of the mountain and they approach Pa with this in mind. However, Pa, who has an illicit still on the mountain, thinks they are revenue men and he and his son Jodie keep them off with a hail of bullets each time they approach.

The Air Force officials enlist the help of Josh Morgan, a 2nd Lt. who was born and raised only 15 miles from the mountain, to help. Josh is captured by the Tatums and they find Josh and Jodie are doubles, and cousins into the bargain. Jodie's two sisters make a play for the dark, handsome Josh and his captain, Robert Salbo. An attractive young typist is also brought on the scene and Jodie decides she is the girl for him.

Pappy Tatum eventually agrees to lease the mountain to the USAF in return for them protecting his still.

ROUSTABOUT (Paramount) 1964

Charlie Rogers—Elvis Presley
Maggie Moore—Barbara Stanwyck
Cathy Lean—Joan Freeman
Joe Lean—Leif Erickson

Producer—Hal Wallis
Director—John Rich

Charlie Rogers is a singer at a tea house in a mid-western State University town, and antagonises some of the student customers with his barbed lyrics which are directed at them. They wait for him outside and a fight starts, but Charlie is a Karate expert and the police arrive and he lands in jail. Marge, a waitress at the café, is attracted to Charlie and bails him out the next day, but Charlie sets off on his motor bike for pastures new.

He joins a run-down carnival owned by Maggie Moore, and meets Cathy, the daughter of the surly Joe Lean who runs the carnival for Maggie. Maggie is deeply in debt and the carnival is not paying. Charlie is a sort of Roustabout, or handyman, around the place, and one day with no work to do he breaks into song. When the young people hear of Charlie's singing they flock to the carnival and things start looking up for Maggie. However, after a series of misunderstandings brought on by a palmist who is jealous of Charlie's attentions to Cathy, Charlie leaves and goes to work for a rival carnival. He is a sensation there, but Cathy comes on the scene to try and get him back.

When Charlie returns however, Joe starts a fight not knowing of Charlie's Karate experience and he gets a good beating up from Charlie. When he realises that Charlie will save the carnival however, he changes his mind about him and the film ends on a rousing note with a happy future assured.

GIRL HAPPY (M.G.M.) 1965

Rusty Wells—Elvis Presley
Valerie—Shelley Fabares
Big Frank—Harold J. Stone
Andy—Gary Crosby

Producer—Joe Pasternak
Director—Boris Segal

Although quite an enjoyable film, the story had only a weak plot and there were no outstanding hits amongst the songs. Elvis plays the part of Rusty Wells, who with his group sings in a night club owned by Big Frank. They are ordered by him to chaperone his daughter on a holiday in Florida (unknown to Valerie, of course). Rusty's own love life is complicated by him having to keep an ever-watchful eye on Valerie, but this is resolved when he and Valerie fall in love. However when Valerie learns that Rusty has been told to watch over her she is furious, she has too much to drink and starts to strip in a nightclub. She is arrested and Rusty attempts a rescue by tunnelling into the jail. Her father meanwhile has bailed her out so Rusty spends the night in jail and escapes the next day dressed as a woman. Valerie realises that Rusty really loves her and they are reunited.

TICKLE ME (Allied Artists) 1965

Lonnie Beale—Elvis Presley
Vera Radford—Julie Adams
Pam Merritt—Jocelyn Lane
Stanley Potter—Jack Mullaney

Producer—Ben Schwalb
Director—Norman Taurog

In this comedy thriller Elvis plays the part of a singing cowboy, Lonnie Beale. He takes a job looking after horses on a health farm for women and is a hit with the ladies from the start, all except Pam Merritt, the PT instructor, who resists his charms. Pam's grandfather has left a fortune in gold in a nearby ghost town and has left Pam a curiously worded letter telling her where to find it. When a masked intruder is surprised by Pam in her bedroom, Lonnie comes to the rescue and Pam warms a little towards him. However, she finds him kissing another girl and is furious. Lonnie leaves and goes back to rodeos but can't forget Pam.

His friend Stan fetches him back and together they follow Pam to the deserted town. There is a storm, Pam is frightened and Lonnie is able to put things right between them. They are surprised by two intruders and Stan falls into the cellar. Lonnie tackles the intruders and rescues Stan who has accidentally discovered the gold in the cellar. Lonnie and Pam are married a few days later.

HARUM SCARUM (M.G.M.) 1965

(Retitled UK—Harem Holiday)

Johnny Tyrone—Elvis Presley
Princess Shalimar—Mary Ann Mobley
Aishah—Fran Jeffries
Prince Dragma—Michael Ansara

Producer—Sam Katzman
Director—Gene Nelson

Not one of Elvis' best films but a lighthearted entertainment. Johnny Tyrone is a motion picture and recording star. On a tour of the Middle East he is kidnapped by a band of assassins who are intent on killing the King. Johnny escapes and meets a beautiful girl who says she is a slave—in reality she is the Princess Shalimar, daughter of the King. Johnny has made friends with a court troupe—including dancing girls and a midget—and when the assassins recapture him, they force him to agree to kill the King in return for the safety of his friends. Johnny has to agree to fall in with their plans, but the Princess and the troupe of friends manage to come to his aid and the King is saved. All ends happily when they all go to the night club Johnny is due to appear at and the lovely Princess gets a kiss from Johnny.

FRANKIE AND JOHNNY (United Artists) 1966

Johnny—Elvis Presley
Frankie—Donna Douglas
Nellie Bly—Nancy Kovack
Clint Braden—Anthony Eisley

Producer—Edward Small
Director—Frederick De Cordova

Frankie and Johnny earn their living by singing on a Mississippi showboat. Frankie loves Johnny but he has a weakness for gambling away their money and she will not marry him because of this. A fortune-teller tells Johnny a red-head will bring him luck and when this red-head turns up in the form of Nellie Bly, Johnny is convinced his luck will change.

Their boss Clint is in love with Nellie however, and is jealous. Johnny wins a large sum of money but Frankie throws it away. Clint's bodyguard, trying to help win Nellie back for his boss, substitutes a live bullet for a dummy one in a gun Frankie uses in their act to "kill" Johnny. Luckily the bullet strikes one of Johnny's lucky mascots, saving his life. Relieved, Frankie realises she loves Johnny no matter what faults he has and all the misunderstandings are eventually sorted out.

PARADISE HAWAIIAN STYLE (Paramount) 1966

Rick Richards—Elvis Presley
Judy Hudson—Suzanna Leigh
Danny Kohana—James Shigeta

Producer—Hal Wallis
Director—Michael Moore

Rick Richards is a pilot who can't keep out of trouble. Out of a job, he returns home to Hawaii and looks up an old friend who has just started up in a flying business of his own. Danny knows of Rick's weakness for pretty girls and the trouble he gets into, so is not very enthusiastic when Rick suggests they work together.

However, he decides to give it a try and Rick persuades all his girl friends who work in local hotels to recruit passengers for the air service. Judy Hudson joins them as a Girl Friday and is not very impressed by Rick, especially when he nearly crashes his helicopter one day whilst carrying a cargo of excited dogs.

One day Rick takes Danny's nine-year-old daughter Jan, and Lani (who has romantic intentions towards Rick) on a joyride. They lose the ignition key and are forced to spend the night on a beach. Danny finds them the next day and furiously tells Rick the partnership is at an end. When Rick returns to Hawaii Judy tells him the others never arrived back. Although Rick stands to lose his licence if he flies again without permission, he and Judy set off to find them. They find Danny with a broken leg and the helicopter damaged.

As usual Rick wins through, he does not lose his licence after all, and meanwhile Judy has fallen in love with him.

SPINOUT (M.G.M.) 1966

(Retitled UK—California Holiday)

Mike McCoy—Elvis Presley	Producer—Joe Pasternak
Cynthia Foxhugh—Shelley Fabares	Director—Norman Taurog
Diana St. Clare—Diane McBain	

Although not one of Elvis' outstanding successes, *Spinout* is an entertaining family film.

Elvis plays Mike McCoy who as well as being a singer with his own band, is also an outstanding racing driver. He is being pursued by three girls, each with a view to matrimony. Cynthia Foxhugh is the daughter of a millionaire; Diane St. Clare, an author; and Mike's own drummer, a plain girl called Les.

Cynthia's father wants Mike to drive his latest racing car in a road race, he also uses all his influence to try and get the band to play at a party for Cynthia when they are booked elsewhere. Mike manages to keep one jump ahead of the amorous females, finally marrying them off to the three beaus who have been pursuing them. He resists the pressures being put on him by the millionaire and wins the race in another car.

EASY COME, EASY GO (Paramount) 1967

Ted Jackson—Elvis Presley	Producer—Hal Wallis
Whitehead—Mickey Elley	Director—John Rich
Tompkins—Reed Morgan	

Whilst de-activating an old underwater mine, Lt. Ted Jackson, a diver in the Navy, sees an old chest in the wreck of a sunken ship. He later asks a local expert, hippie Jo Symington, for information about the ship, pretending he is writing a manual. She tells him that the ship carried a chest of pieces of eight. Upon his discharge from the Navy Ted goes after the treasure but finds someone else already after it. After some under-water excitement with the two rivals going to extremes to out-do each other, the chest is finally brought to the surface but is found to be full of copper coins and virtually worthless. The money is used as a down payment on an art centre for Jo, and Ted returns to sing at the Easy Go-Go, a dockside disco.

DOUBLE TROUBLE (M.G.M.) 1967

Guy Lambert—Elvis Presley	Producers—Judd Bernard/Irwin Winkler
Jill Conway—Annette Day	Director—Norman Taurog
Gerald Waverley—John Williams	
Claire Dunham—Yvonne Romain	

Guy Lambert is a young bachelor who sings in a London discotheque, and he is being pursued by two girls, Jill, a young heiress, and Claire, a sophisticated playgirl. In an extremely complicated plot, Jill is sent to Belgium at the same time as Guy is there for an engagement. Jill is nearly murdered, and Guy is nearly drowned.

In the events which follow, Jill's Uncle Gerald arrives to protect her, thinks Guy has kidnapped her and has him arrested, so leaving the way open for the real kidnappers. After a series of adventures, each more complicated than the last, Guy and Jill set sail for England thinking all is well only to be caught up in even more chaos and confusion.

CLAMBAKE (United Artists) 1967

Scott Heywood—Elvis Presley	Producer—Levy-Gardner-Laven Productions
Dianne Carter—Shelley Fabares	Director—Arthur Nadel
Tom Wilson—Will Hutchins	
James Jamison—Bill Bixby	
Duster Heywood—James Gregory	
Sam Burton—Gary Merrill	

Duster Heywood is a millionaire who owns the Duster Oil Company. He is ambitious for his son Scott to take on responsibilities in the company but Scott wants to stand on his own feet and is tired of his life of luxury, preferring to work in the research laboratory.

Needing time to think out his future, he drives away one day with nowhere particular in mind. He meets Tom Wilson some days later and in conversation they decide to swap identities. Scott drives off on Tom's motor bike to take up a job as water ski instructor at Miami Beach. Once there and established as Tom Wilson, he meets Dianne Carter, who is out to get herself a husband, James Jamison, a rich playboy. She enlists Scott's help in hooking the playboy, but Scott becomes jealous as he is himself attracted to Dianne.

Wanting to impress Dianne he pursuades a rival boat-owner to let him fix a fault on his boat's hull with a compound he has developed himself. He then drives the boat in a race and of course wins the race and the girl.

SPEEDWAY (M.G.M.) 1968

Steve Gregson—Elvis Presley	Producer—Douglas Laurence
Susan Jacks—Nancy Sinatra	Director—Norman Taurog

Steve Gregson is a successful champion motor racer who always has plenty of cash due to his winning so many races. His friend Kenny Dow is his manager but is very irresponsible. Steve will help anyone in need of money and is generous to a fault. Unfortunately, due to his high earnings, his generosity in handing out money and Kenny's lack of knowledge of tax forms, Steve finds he is 100,000 dollars in debt to the Internal Revenue.

A young accountant, Susan Jacks is assigned to handle his money and although they are attracted to each other, the differences in their personalities come between them.

As his debts pile up the only solution seems to be to sell his beloved racing car but Susan negotiates an extension to paying back his tax and he is able to enter the Daytona 500 race only to crash just before the finishing line.

STAY AWAY JOE (M.G.M.) 1968

Joe Lightcloud—Elvis Presley	Producer—Douglas Laurence
Glenda Callahan—Joan Blondell	Director—Peter Tewksbury
Charlie Lightcloud—Burgess Meredith	
Annie Lightcloud—Katy Jurado	

A film with not much point and even less of a story. Joe Lightcloud who lives on an Indian reservation is given $20 and a young bull by the government to enable him to start a herd. Joe however prefers to spend his time enjoying himself—fighting, singing, riding bulls and motor bikes.

After a wild party in which Joe's bull mistakenly gets killed for food, he eventually raises enough money for a new one by selling his car. Catastrophe follows catastrophe, and the film ends with a wild fight and Joe's house collapsing around him.

LIVE A LITTLE, LOVE A LITTLE (M.G.M.) 1968

Greg Nolan—Elvis Presley	Producer—Douglas Laurence
Bernice—Michele Carey	Director—Norman Taurog
Harry—Dick Sargent	
Mike Lansdown—Don Porter	
Penlow—Rudy Vallee	

Greg Nolan, a newspaper photographer, gets mixed up with a pretty girl, Bernice, and a Great Dane called Albert. When he gets pneumonia, Bernice looks after him but meanwhile he has lost his job. She moves him into her apartment, and he manages to get two jobs with very different bosses, so Greg is constantly changing his appearance.

After moving to a new house with only one bedroom Bernice runs away but is chased and caught by Greg who tells her he loves her. All ends happily for the three of them.

THE TROUBLE WITH GIRLS (M.G.M.) 1969

Walter Hale—Elvis Presley	Producer—Lester Welch
Nita—Sheree North	Director—Peter Tewksbury
Johnny Anthony—Edward Andrews	
Charlene—Marlyn Mason	

One of the big events of the year to the people of Radford Centre is the arrival of the chatauqua—a travelling academy—"The Rolling Canvas College". Its manager is Walter Hale who grew up with the Centre as a singer. One of the performers is Charlene, a pretty girl who is always fighting for good causes. She and Walter always seem to be in conflict, but there is also a mutual admiration between them.

The happy atmosphere of the chatauqua impresses the people of Radford—some see it as an escape from the small town life.

There is trouble however when the town pharmacist is murdered and the wrong man is arrested. Walter manages to solve the mystery and turns his last show into a public unmasking of the murderer and all ends happily.

CHARRO (National General) 1969

Jess Wade—Elvis Presley   Producer/Director—Charles M. Warren
Tracy—Ina Balin
Vince—Victor French

Jess Wade is a former outlaw who has gone straight for almost a year. His former outlaw friends trap him and show him a victory cannon they have stolen from Mexico. Wade tells them they will be hunted down but Vince, the leader of the gang, shows him a poster they have circulated which claims that it is Jess who is wanted for the theft. The poster describes a scar on his neck that he is supposed to have received during the robbery. The gang then scar him with a hot poker and leave him helpless in the wilderness.

When he recovers he makes his way to the only town where he knows he will be safe, and where the sheriff is a friend of his. This man is Dan Ramsey, who has known Wade since he was a boy, and he has refused to display the "wanted" poster.

The plot intensifies when Vince's brother is captured by Jess after injuring the sheriff and Vince threatens to destroy the town with the cannon unless his brother is released.

After some fierce fighting in which many of the gang are killed and Vince's brother is crushed to death by the cannon, Jess wins through and the film ends with him taking the cannon and the outlaw back to justice.

CHANGE OF HABIT (Universal) 1969

Dr. John Carpenter—Elvis Presley   Producer—Joe Connelly
Sister Michelle—Mary Tyler Moore   Director—William Graham
Sister Irene—Barbra McNair
Sister Barbara—Jane Elliot

A change of role from Elvis' usual playboy ones, also a higher standard of acting in this film in which Elvis plays the part of a doctor. Three nuns are sent to assist Dr. John Carpenter at his surgery in a New York ghetto with a tough mixed population. The nuns do not wear habits and Dr. Carpenter is unaware of their calling.

Father Gibbons, the local priest, however, is aware of this, and does not approve of the methods used by the Catholic Action Committee in sending the girls to this district, nor does he approve of their new ideas.

Coloured Irene runs into colour problems on her house calls and also the local protection racket.

Barbara finds she cannot come to terms with her political beliefs and her religious ones.

Michelle—in close contact with Dr. John—realises he is falling in love with her and tries to rebuff him.

The three girls organise a Fiesta and after some trouble are ordered to go back to the Convent. Barbara decides she cannot return and stays to help the people. Irene and Michelle do return to the convent but Michelle is obviously attracted to Dr. John and at a service in which she goes to hear him sing her mind is obviously in conflict. The film ends with nothing resolved.

ELVIS—THAT'S THE WAY IT IS (M.G.M.) 1970

(Documentary)   Producer—Dale Hutchinson
     Director—Denis Sanders

A full-length documentary with plenty of songs for the Elvis fan. The film shows Elvis in rehearsal, fooling around, and relaxing. Fans are interviewed and the 1970 Fan Convention in Luxembourg is also shown.

We see Elvis rehearsing on M.G.M.'s sound stage, rehearsing in the hotel, and in a private room.

Waiters and hotel managers are interviewed and the hotel prepared for the great star.

The cameras show Elvis in concerts in Las Vegas and Phoenix.

Compiled by
TODD
SLAUGHTER

Although not a candid documentary of the personal side of Elvis' life, the fans received it enthusiastically and the film shows that Elvis is still a dynamic and exciting performer.

ELVIS ON TOUR (M.G.M.) 1972

(Documentary)

Producer—Pierre Adidge
Director—Robert Abel

This is a documentary of four dates played on a tour of 15 concerts in as many days.

We first see Elvis nervous and ignoring his comedian's banter as he awaits his call. A few pre-recorded comments are heard from Elvis before he actually starts. After an abrupt cut to a studio to demonstrate how they can improve on *Separate Ways* we are whisked off by plane and car to another engagement.

We see once again, hotel preparations, various film clips and screen embraces, and a humorous set of stage shots.

Elvis is filmed in Virginia, and at the famous New York Press Conference. During this time short film clips of Graceland are shown.

In conclusion we see Elvis relaxing in his car whilst *Memories* is played, and we get a glimpse of Elvis the man. A film to see twice over if possible, and to see the proof and the performance and talent that have made Elvis into a legend and a King.

WIDE-SCREEN CROSSWORD *Answers on page 62*

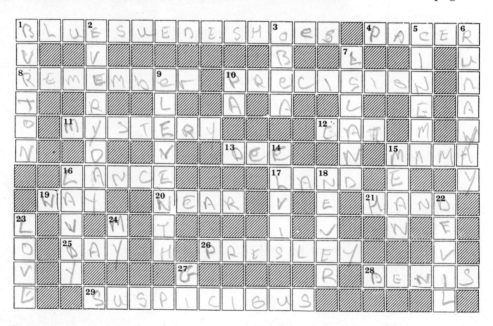

ACROSS
1   Don't step on Elvis' (4, 5, 5).
4   & 1 Down. Elvis' screen name in *Flaming Star*.
8   I'll — you from *Aloha from Hawaii*.
10   — Tool Company. Elvis' first employers.
11   — *Train*.
12   The Hillbilly — (nickname).
13   Elvis' stepmother.
15   She liked the roses.
16   First name of Elvis' "Stand In" in *Roustabout*.
17   *Promised* —.
19   Elvis sang it: *His* — from *Aloha from Hawaii*.
20   We all wish Elvis was this.
21   Female fans wish Elvis was in their.
25   *Any* — *now* from *Elvis in Memphis*.
26   See 14 Down.
28   First name of Director of TTWII.
29   They can't live with these minds.

DOWN
1   See 4 Across.
2   *If* — *was like Christmas*.
3   This word was omitted from Elvis' marriage to Priscilla.
5   Elvis went there when *That's Alright Mama* was first played.
6   Del Shannon song from *On Stage*.
7   — *of Love* from *Blue Hawaii*.
9   *Girls! Girls! Girls!* was Elvis' — movie.
10   Lisa never calls Elvis this.
14   & 26 Across. Our King.
15   — *Woman Blues*.
16   Mawldy Ciss (anag) name the rest of song title.
18   We all hope Elvis will be — *Ending*.
22   She was like an angel with her disguise.
23   These letters came straight from the heart.
24   — *Boy*.
27   Elvis was this from 1958–1960.

FROM `DOWN-UNDER´

I have now been affiliated with the Elvis Presley Fan Club of Victoria for almost 13 years as a member, committee member and then as President. In those 13 years the club has continued to expand, thus creating more work with each week, but I have never regretted becoming involved in something which gives little reward except personal satisfaction and hope I will be involved for many years to come.

My own interest in Elvis began back in 1957 at age eight after seeing a preview of *Jailhouse Rock* at a Melbourne theatre and has never looked back since. Of course my mother was, and still is, an avid Elvis fan, something which gave constant fuel to my interest in those early days. From my first record my Elvis collection has grown over the years to some 335 LPs and 416 45s and 78s at the time of writing. Although Elvis fan clubs were in operation in the Melbourne area in the late 50s (by the early 1960s there were none) I did not take part in that facet of the Elvis world until the EPFCOV started up in 1964 under Gaye Paton.

In those days the club was called the "Proudly For Presley Fan Club of Australia" and remained as such until 1967 when Gaye handed the club over to my wife-to-be Gina. The highlight of those first three years was undoubtedly the club's involvement in Melbourne's 1966 Moomba Parade which created a great amount of publicity for Elvis, RCA and the club.

From 1967 through to '71 the club was closely associated with a 1950s rock 'n' roll dance called the "Melbourne Jailhouse" and it was from this dance that we drew the hardcore of our membership. It was also during this period that I personally became more involved in the club, firstly as a committee member and then as President. Unfortunately this association with the dance came to an end in '71 due to the dance's closure and it was not until 1976 that we were in a position to again become involved in rock 'n' roll dances, helped greatly by the current resurgence of interest in and appreciation of the 50s era.

Since 1971 the club has gone from strength to strength and has received tremendous support from its members. Movie nights, interstate trips, Christmas parties, etc have all met with great success, enabling the club to continue and expand as well as netting profits for various charities here. The club has maintained a strong identification with the early Elvis over the past seven years and this policy of promoting the memory of the early days has become an integral part of the functioning of the EPFCOV. We are in the process of building up a club film library which was started some time back with the purchase of El's finest film *King Creole*.

Products such as Elvis T-shirts, stickers, photos, badges, matches, stationery, etc are available to members through the club as well as books and records.

My wife Gina and I spent a month in the States in 1971 and a further three months in 1973 but, although we visited each of the 50 states, so fulfilling a lifelong ambition and meeting many wonderful people, we failed to catch an Elvis show. Naturally we visited "Graceland" and El's birthplace in Tupelo, Mississippi but the Elvis concert remained elusive. However, as I write, we are preparing to catch that elusive concert in San Francisco later this month, due to the help of Stateside member Hedy Drissen to whom we will long be grateful.

I would like to finish up by thanking all those members who have supported the club over the past 13 years, in particular my wife Gina, Roger and Joan Hammond, Keith Asbury, Maree Paynting and Adrian Rossi for their help in running the club, to Todd Slaughter for inviting me to do this article and of course to Elvis A. Presley who has given to many millions so much pleasure over the past 22 years.

Wayne Hawthorne,
President,
The Elvis Presley Fan Club of Victoria,
PO Box 82,
Elsternwick, Victoria 3185,
AUSTRALIA.

Elvis RCA Records and Tapes Catalogue

ELVIS FOR EVERYONE
Your cheatin' heart & Wild in the country & Finders keepers, losers weepers (with *The Jordanaires*): In my way: Tomorrow night: Memphis, Tennessee & For the millionth and the last time (with *The Jordanaires*): Forget me never: Sound advice: Santa Lucia & I met her today (with *The Jordanaires*): When it rains, it really pours
(s)SF 8323 (LP) **P8S 11617** (S8) **PK 11617** (C)

ELVIS' GOLDEN RECORDS—VOL. 1
Hound dog: I love you because: All shook up: Heartbreak Hotel: You're a heartbreaker: Love me: Too much: Don't be cruel: That's when your heartaches begin: I'll never let you go: Love me tender: I forgot to remember to forget: Anyway you want me (that's how I will be): I want you, I need you, I love you (with *The Jordanaires*)
(s)SF 8129 (e) (LP) **P8S 11602** (S8) **PK 11602** (C)

ELVIS' GOLDEN RECORDS—VOL. 2
I need your love tonight: Don't: Wear my ring around your neck: My wish came true: I got stung: Lov'ng you: (Let me be your) Teddy bear: One night: A big hunk o' love: I beg of you: A fool such as I: Doncha' think it's time: Jailhouse rock: Treat me nice (with *The Jordanaires*)
(s)SF 8151 (LP) **P8S 11531** (S8) **PK 11531** (C)

ELVIS' GOLDEN RECORDS—VOL. 3
It's now or never: Stuck on you: Fame and fortune: I gotta know: Surrender: I feel so bad: Are you lonesome tonight: (Marie's the name) His latest flame: Little sister: Good luck charm: Anything that's part of you: She's not you (with *The Jordanaires*)
(s)SF 7630 (LP) (LSP 2765) **P8S 11570** (S8) **PK 11570** (C)

ELVIS' GOLD RECORDS—VOL. 4
Love letters & Witchcraft & It hurts me (with *The Jordanaires*): What'd I say (with *The Jubilee Four & Carole Lombard Quartet*): Please don't drag that string around (with *The Jordanaires*): Indescribably blue (with *The Jordanaires & The Imperials Quartet*): You're the devil in disguise & Lonely man & A mess of blues & Ask me (with *The Jordanaires*): Ain't that loving you baby: Just tell her Jim said hello (with *The Jordanaires*)
(s)SF 7924 (LP) (LSP 3921) **P8S 11571** (S8) **PK 11571** (C)

ELVIS IS BACK
Make me know it: Fever: The girl of my best friend: I will be home again: Dirty, dirty feeling: The thrill of your love: Soldier boy: Such a night: It feels so right: The girl next door: Like a baby: Reconsider baby (with *The Jordanaires*)
(s)SF 5060 (LP) (LSP 2231) **P8S 11532** (S8) **PK 11532** (C)

ELVIS LIVE AT MADISON SQUARE GARDEN
Introduction: Theme from "2001—A Space Odyssey": That's all right: Proud Mary: Never been to Spain: You don't have to say you love me: You've lost that lovin' feeling': Polk salad Annie: Love me: All shook up: Heartbreak Hotel: Medley: (Let me be your) Teddy bear—Don't be cruel—Love me tender: The impossible dream: Introductions by *Elvis*: Hound dog: Suspicious minds: For the good times: American trilogy: Funny how time slips away: I can't stop loving you: Can't help falling in love
(s)SF 8296 (LP) (LSP 4776) **P8S 2054** (S8) **PK 2054** (C)

ELVIS NOW
Help me make it through the night & Miracle of the rosary (with *The Imperials Quartet*): Hey Jude: Put your hand in the hand & Until it's time for you to go & We can make the morning (with *The Imperials Quartet*): Early mornin' rain (with *The Nashville Edition*): Sylvia: Fools rush in (where angels fear to tread): I was born about ten thousand years ago
(s)SF 8266 (LP) (LSP 4671) **P8S 11612** (S8) **PK 11612** (C)

ELVIS SINGS "FLAMING STAR"
Flaming star: Wonderful world: Night life: All I needed was the rain: Too much monkey business: Yellow rose of Texas: The eyes of Texas: She's a machine: Do the vega: Tiger man
MP8 101 (S8) **MPK 101** (C)

FROM ELVIS IN MEMPHIS
Wearin' that loved on look: Only the strong survive: I'll hold you in my heart: Long black limousine: It keeps right on a-hurtin': I'm moving on: Power of my love: Gentle on my mind: After loving you: True love travels on a gravel road: Any day now: In the Ghetto
(s)SF 8029 (LP) (LSP 4155) **PQ8 1456** (Q8) **P8S 1456** (S8) **VCS 67304** (C)

FROM MEMPHIS TO VEGAS—Elvis at the International Hotel, Las Vegas
Blue suede shoes: Johnny B. Goode & All shook up & Are you lonesome tonight (with *The Sweet Inspirations & The Imperials Quartet*): Hound dog: I can't stop loving you (with *The Sweet Inspirations & The Imperials Quartet*): My babe (with *The Sweet Inspirations*): Medley—Mystery train—Tiger man: Words & In the ghetto & Suspicious minds & Can't help falling in love (with *The Sweet Inspirations & The Imperials Quartet*)*
FROM VEGAS TO MEMPHIS—Elvis back in Memphis
Inherit the wind: This is the story: Stranger in my own home town: A little bit of green: And the grass won't pay no mind: Do you know who I am: From a Jack to a King: The fair's moving on: You'll think of me: Without love (There is nothing)†
(s)SF 8080-1 (LP) (LSP 6020)
(2 records in special folder sleeve with colour photo insert)
***P8S 1634** (S8) ***PK 1634** (C)
†**P8S 1632** (S8) †**PK 1632** (C)

G.I. BLUES (from the original soundtrack)
Tonight is so right for love: What's she really like: Frankfort special: Wooden heart: G.I. blues: Pocketful of rainbows: Shoppin' around: Big boots: Didja' ever: Blue suede shoes: Doin' the best I can (with *The Jordanaires*)
(s)SF 5078 (LP) (LSP 2256) **P8S 5078** (S8) **PK 5078** (C)

GOOD TIMES
Take good care of her: Loving arms: I got a feelin' in my body: If that isn't love: She wears my ring: I've got a thing about you baby: My boy: Spanish eyes: Talk about the good times: Good Time Charlie's got the blues
(s)APL1 0475 (LP) **GG** **APS1 0475** (S8) **SS** **APK1 0475** (C) **MM**

HE TOUCHED ME
He touched me: I've got confidence: Amazing grace (with *The Nashville Edition*): Seeing is believing: He is my everything: Bosom of Abraham: An evening prayer: Lead me, guide me: There is no God but God: A thing called love: I, John: Reach out to Jesus (with *The Imperials Quartet*)
(s)SF 8275 (LP) (LSP 4690) **P8S 1923** (S8) **PK 1923** (C)

HIS HAND IN MINE
His hand in mine: I'm gonna walk dem golden stairs: In my Father's house: Milky white way: Known only to Him: I believe in the man in the sky: Joshua fit the battle: Jesus knows what I need: Swing down sweet chariot: Mansion over the hilltop: If we never meet again: Working on the building (with *The Jordanaires*)
(s)SF 8207 (LP) (LSP 2328) **P8S 11576** (S8) **PK 11576** (C)

HOW GREAT THOU ART as sung by Elvis Presley
How great Thou art: In the garden: Somebody bigger than you and I: Farther along: Stand by me: Without Him: So high: Where could I go but to the Lord: By and by: If the Lord wasn't walking by my side: Run on: Where no one stands alone: Crying in the chapel (with *The Jordanaires & The Imperials Quartet*)
(s)SF 8206 (LP) (LSP 3758) **P8S 11581** (S8) **PK 11581** (C)

I GOT LUCKY
I got lucky (with *The Jordanaires*): What a wonderful life: I need somebody to lean on: Yoga is as yoga does: Riding the rainbow & Fools fall in love (with *The Jordanaires*): The love machine: Home is where the heart is (with *The Jordanaires*): You gotta stop: If you think I don't need you
MP8 151 (S8) **MPK 151** (C)

I'M 10,000 YEARS OLD, ELVIS COUNTRY
Snowbird & Tomorrow never comes (with *The Imperials Quartet*): Little cabin on the hill: Whole lot-ta shakin' goin' on: Funny how time slips away (with *The Imperials Quartet & The Jordanaires*): I really don't want to know & There goes my everything (with *The Imperials Quartet*): It's your baby, you rock it: The fool: Faded love: I washed my hands in muddy water: Make the world go away (with *The Imperials Quartet & The Jordanaires*)
(s)SF 8172 (LP) (LSP 4460)
(Photo insert included with record)
P8S 1655 (S8) **PK 1655** (C)

KING CREOLE (from the original soundtrack)
King Creole: As long as I have you: Hard headed woman: Trouble: Dixieland rock: Don't ask me why: Lover doll: Crawfish: Young dreams: Steadfast, loyal and true: New Orleans (with *The Jordanaires*)
(s)SF 8231 (e) (LP) (LPM 1884) **P8S 11621** (S8) **PK 11621** (C)

LET'S BE FRIENDS
Stay away Joe: If I'm a fool (for loving you): Let's be friends: *Let's forget about the stars: *Mama: I'll be there (if you ever want me): Almost: Change of habit: Have a happy
(*these tracks are recorded in mono)
MP8 138 (S8) **MPK 138** (C)

LOVE LETTERS FROM ELVIS
Love letters: When I'm over you (with *The Imperials Quartet & The Jordanaires*): If I were you (with *The Imperials Quartet*): Got my mojo working: Heart of Rome: Only believe (with *The Imperials Quartet*): This is our dance: Cindy, Cindy: I'll never know (with *The Imperials Quartet*): It ain't no big thing (but it's growing) (with *The Nashville Edition*): Life
(s)SF 8202 (LP) (LSP 4530) **P8S 11575** (S8) **PK 11575** (C)

ON STAGE FEBRUARY 1970—Elvis at the International Hotel, Las Vegas
See see rider blues: Release me (and let me love again): Sweet Caroline: Runaway: The wonder of you: Polk salad Annie: Yesterday: Proud Mary: Walk a mile in my shoes: Let it be me (Je t'appartiens) (with *The Imperials Quartet*)
(s)SF 8128 (LP) (LSP 4362)
(4-colour poster insert included with record)
PQ8 1594 (Q8) **P8S 1594** (S8) **PK 1594** (C)

RAISED ON ROCK
Raised on rock: Are you sincere (with *Voice*): Find out what's happening (with *J. D. Sumner & The Stamps*): I miss you (with *Voice*): Girl of mine (with *J. D. Sumner & The Stamps*): For ol' time's sake: If you don't come back: Just a little bit: Sweet Angeline (with *Voice*): Three corn patches (with *J. D. Sumner & The Stamps*)
(s)APL1 0388 (LP **GG** **APS1 0388** (S8) **SS** **APK1 0388** (C) **MM**

ROCK 'N' ROLL
Blue suede shoes: I got a sweetie (I got a woman): I'm counting on you: I'm left, you're right, she's gone: That's all right: Money honey: Mystery train: I'm gonna sit right down and cry over you: Trying to get you: One-sided love affair: Lawdy Miss Clawdy: Shake rattle and roll
(s)SF 8233 (e) (LP) **P8S 11620** (S8) **PK 11620** (C)

SOMETHING FOR EVERYBODY
There's always me: Give me the right: It's a sin: Sentimental me: Starting today: Gently: I'm coming home: In your arms: Put the blame on me: Judy: I want you with me: I slipped, I stumbled, I fell (with *The Jordanaires*)
(s)SF 5106 (LP) (LSP 2370) **P8S 11604** (S8) **PK 11604** (C)

THAT'S THE WAY IT IS
I just can't help believin' (with *The Imperials Quartet & The Sweet Inspirations*): Twenty days and twenty nights: How the web was woven: Patch it up (with *The Imperials Quartet & The Sweet Inspirations*): Mary in the morning (with *The Imperials Quartet*): You don't have to say you love me: You've lost that lovin' feelin' & I've lost you (with *The Imperials Quartet & The Sweet Inspirations*): Just pretend: Stranger in the crowd: The next step is love: Bridge over troubled water (with *The Imperials Quartet & The Sweet Inspirations*)
(s)SF 8162 (LP) (LSP 4445) **PQ8 1652** (Q8) **P8S 11566** (S8) **PK 11566** (C)

WORLD WIDE 50 GOLD AWARD HITS—VOL. 1
Heartbreak Hotel: I was the one: I want you, I need you, I love you: Don't be cruel: Hound dog: Love me tender: Anyway you want me (that's how I will be): Too much & Playing for keeps & All shook up & That's when your heartaches begin & Loving you (with *The Jordanaires*): (Let me be your) Teddy bear (with *The Jordanaires*): Jailhouse rock: Treat me nice: I beg of you & Don't & Wear my ring around your neck & Hard headed woman (with *The Jordanaires*): I got stung: (Now and then there's) A fool such as I & A big hunk o' love & Stuck on you & A mess of blues & It's now or never (with *The Jordanaires*): I gotta know & Are you lonesome tonight & Surrender (with *The Jordanaires*): I feel so bad: Little sister: Can't help falling in love & Rock-a-hula baby & Anything that's part of you & Good luck charm & She's not you & Return to sender & Where do you come from? (with *The Jordanaires*): One broken

heart for sale (with *The Mello Men*): You're the devil in disguise & Bossa nova baby & Kissin' cousins & Viva Las Vegas (with *The Jordanaires*): Ain't that loving you baby: Wooden heart: Crying in the chapel (with *The Jordanaires*): If I can dream: In the ghetto: Suspicious minds: Don't cry daddy: Kentucky rain: Excerpt from a Press interview with Elvis at the time of his sailing in the *U.S.S. Randall*

(m)LPM 6401 (LP) (LPM 6401)
(4 records in box with photograph album)

WORLD WIDE 25 GOLD AWARD HITS—VOL. 1
Heartbreak Hotel: I was the one: I want you, I need you, I love you: A mess of blues (with *The Jordanaires*): Hound dog: Love me tender: Anyway you want me (that's how I will be): A big hunk o' love & Playing for keeps & All shook up & That's when your heartaches begin & Loving you & (Let me be your) Teddy bear (with *The Jordanaires*): Jailhouse rock: I got stung: I beg of you & Don't & Wear my ring around your neck & Hard headed woman (with *The Jordanaires*): Don't be cruel: Too much (with *The Jordanaires*): Treat me nice: (Now and then there's) A fool such as I & Stuck on you & It's now or never (with *The Jordanaires*)
DPT8 5000 (S8) **DPTK 5000** (C)

WORLD WIDE 25 GOLD AWARD HITS—VOL. 2
Are you lonesome tonight & I gotta know (with *The Jordanaires*): I feel so bad: Surrender (with *The Jordanaires*): Don't cry daddy: Kentucky rain: Little sister: Can't help falling in love & Rock-a-hula baby & Anything that's part of you & Good luck charm & She's not you & Return to sender & Where do you come from? & Bossa nova baby & Kissin' cousins & Viva Las Vegas (with *The Jordanaires*): Ain't that loving you baby: Crying in the chapel (with *The Jordanaires*): In the ghetto: If I can dream: One broken heart for sale (with *The Mello Men*): You're the devil in disguise (with *The Jordanaires*): Wooden heart: Suspicious minds: Excerpts from a Press interview with Elvis at the time of his sailing in the *U.S.S. Randall*
DPTB 5001 (S8) **DPTK 5001** (C)

WORLD WIDE 25, GOLD AWARD HITS—VOL. 3
Rip it up: Paralysed: Love me: We're gonna move: Poor boy: Hot Dog & New Orleans & Dixieland rock (with *The Jordanaires*): Crawfish: Don't ask me why & King Creole (with *The Jordanaires*): One night: His latest flame (Marie's the name): They remind me too much of you (with *The Mello Men*): Young and beautiful & Fame and fortune & Lonely man & Witchcraft & It hurts me & Puppet on a string & I believe in the man in the sky (with *The Jordanaires*): Any day now: I've lost you & Patch it up (with *The Imperials Quartet & The Sweet Inspirations*): There goes my everything (with *The Imperials Quartet*)
DPT8 5011 (S8) **DPTK 5011** (C)

WORLD WIDE 25 GOLD AWARD HITS—VOL. 4
My baby left me: When my blue moon turns to gold again: Mean woman blues & Lonesome cowboy (with *The Jordanaires*): Got a lot o' livin' to do: Young dreams (with *The Jordanaires*): Trouble: As long as I have you (with *The Jordanaires*): Lover doll: Don'cha think it's time & My wish came true (with *The Jordanaires*): Wild in the country: (You're so square) Baby I don't care & I want to be free & I need your love tonight & Just tell her Jim said hello & Ask me & Tell me why (with *The Jordanaires*): The wonder of you (with *The Imperials Quartet*): Please don't drag that string around (with *The Jordanaires*): You'll think of me: The next step is love: You don't have to say you love me: I really don't want to know (with *The Imperials Quartet*)
DPT8 5012 (S8) **DPTK 5012** (C)

ALOHA FROM HAWAII—VOL. 1
Theme from "2001—A Space Odyssey": See see rider: Burning love: Something: You gave me a mountain: Steamroller blues: My way: Love me: Johnny B. Goode: It's over: Blue suede shoes: I'm so lonesome I could cry: I can't stop loving you: Hound dog (introduction by *Elvis Presley*: vocal accompaniments by *J. D. Sumner & The Stamps, Kathy Westmoreland & The Sweet Inspirations)*
PQ8 2140 (Q8)

ALOHA FROM HAWAII—VOL. 2
What now my love: Fever: Welcome to my world: Suspicious minds: I'll remember you: Medley—Long tall Sally/Whole lotta shakin' goin' on: American trilogy: A big hunk o' love: Can't help falling in love (introductions by *Elvis Presley*: vocal accompaniments by *J. D. Sumner & The Stamps, Kathy Westmoreland & The Sweet Inspirations)*
PQ8 2141 (Q8)

ELVIS
Fool & Where do I go from here (with *J. D. Sumner & The Stamps*): Love me, love the life I lead: It's still here: It's impossible (with *The Sweet Inspirations & J. D. Sumner & The Stamps*): For lovin' you (with *The Nashville Edition*): Padre: I'll take you home again, Kathleen: I will be true: Don't think twice, it's all right
SF 8378
APS1 0283 (S8) **SS** **APK1 0283** (C) **MM**

ELVIS' CHRISTMAS ALBUM
Blue Christmas: Silent Night: White Christmas: Santa Claus is back in town: I'll be home for Christmas: If every day was like Christmas (with *The Jordanaires & The Imperials Quartet*): Here comes Santa Claus (down Santa Claus Lane): O little town of Bethlehem: Santa bring my baby back (to me): Mama liked the roses
MP8 232 (S8) **MPK 232** (C)

THE ELVIS PRESLEY SUN COLLECTION
That's all right mama: Blue moon of Kentucky: I don't care if the sun don't shine: Good rockin' tonight: Milk cow blues boogie: You're a heartbreaker: I'm left, you're right, she's gone: Baby let's play house: Mystery train: I forgot to remember to forget: I'll never let you go: I love you because (1st version): Tryin' to get to you: Blue moon: Just because: I love you because (2nd version)
(m)HY 1001 (LP) **TT**
HY8 1001 (S8) **TT** **HYK 1001** (C) **TT**

HAVING FUN WITH ELVIS ON STAGE
Elvis talking to and with his concert audiences—seldom seen insights into the warmth, the humour and the electricity of a live Elvis Presley performance
(m)APM1 0818 (LP) (CPM1 0818) **GG**

HITS OF THE 70s
The wonder of you: I'm leavin': Burning love: Always on my mind: I just can't help believing: You don't have to say you love me: There goes my everything: Rags to riches: Until it's time for you to go: Kentucky rain: I've lost you: An American trilogy
(m)/(s)LP1 7527 (LP) **GG**
LPS1 7527 (S8) **SS** **LPK1 7527** (C) **MM**

ELVIS LIVE AT MADISON SQUARE GARDEN
Introduction: Theme from "2001—A Space Odyssey": That's all right: Proud Mary: Never been to Spain: You don't have to say you love me: You've lost that lovin' feelin': Polk salad Annie: Love me: All shook up: Heartbreak Hotel: Medley—(Let me be your) Teddy bear/Don't be cruel/Love me tender: The impossible dream: Introduction by *Elvis*: Hound dog: Suspicious minds: For the good times: American trilogy: Funny how time slips away: I can't stop loving you: Can't help falling in love
PO8 2054 (Q8)

PROMISED LAND
Promised land: There's a honky tonk angel (who will take me back in) (with *Voice*): Help me (with *Voice & J. D. Sumner & The Stamps*): Mr. Songman (with *Voice*): Love song of the year & It's midnight & Your love's been a long time coming (with *Voice & J. D. Sumner & The Stamps*): If you talk in your sleep: Thinking about you & You ask me to (with *Voice & J. D. Sumner & The Stamps*)
(s)APL1 0873 (LP) **HH**
APS1 0873 (S8) **SS** **APK1 0873** (C) **MM**

ALMOST IN LOVE
Almost in love: Long legged girl (with the short dress on) (with *The Jordanaires*): Edge of reality: My little friend: A little less conversation: Rubberneckin': Clean up your own back yard: U.S. male (with *The Jordanaires*): Charro: Stay away, Joe
MP8 121 (S8) **MPK 121** (C)

ALOHA FROM HAWAII VIA SATELLITE
Theme from "2001—A Space Odyssey": See see rider: Burning love: Something: You gave me a mountain: Steamroller blues: My way: Love me: Johnny B. Goode: It's over: Blue suede shoes: I'm so lonesome I could cry: I can't stop loving you: Hound dog: What now my love: Fever: Welcome to my world: Suspicious minds: I'll remember you: Medley—Long tall Sally/Whole lotta shakin' goin' on: American trilogy: A big hunk o' love: Can't help falling in love (introductions by *Elvis Presley*: vocal accompaniments by *J. D. Sumner & The Stamps, Kathy Westmoreland & The Sweet Inspirations)*
(s)DPS 2940 (LP) (VPSX 6089)
(2 records in special folder sleeve)
P8S 5144 (S8) **PK 5144** (C)

BLUE HAWAII (from the original soundtrack)
Blue Hawaii: Almost always true: Aloha-oe: No more: Can't help falling in love: Rock-a-hula baby: Moonlight swim: Ku-u-i-po (Hawaiian sweetheart): Ito eats: Slicin' sand: Hawaiian sunset: Beach boy blues: Island of love: Hawaiian wedding song (with *The Jordanaires)*
(s)SF 8145 (LP) (LSP 2426)
P8S 11561 (S8) **PK 11561** (C)

C'MON EVERYBODY
C'mon everybody (with *The Jordanaires*): Angel: Easy come, easy go: A whistling tune (with *The Jordanaires*): Follow that dream: King of the whole wide world (with *The Jordanaires*): I'll take love: Today, tomorrow and forever (with *The Jordanaires*): I'm not the marrying kind: This is living (with *The Jordanaires)*
MP8 143 (S8) **MPK 143** (C)

BURNING LOVE AND HITS FROM HIS MOVIES—VOL. 2
Burning love (with *J. D. Sumner & The Stamps*): Tender feeling (from "Kissin' Cousins") & Am I ready (from "Spinout") & Tonight is so right for love (from "G.I. Blues") (with *The Jordanaires*): Guadalajara (from "Fun in Acapulco") (with *The Jordanaires & The Amigos*): It's a matter of time (with *J. D. Sumner & The Stamps*): No more (from "Blue Hawaii"): Santa Lucia (from "Viva Las Vegas") (with *The Jordanaires*): We'll be together (from "Girls! Girls! Girls!") (with *The Amigos*): I love only one girl (from "Double Trouble") (with *J. D. Sumner & The Stamps*)
MP8 162 (S8) **MPK 162** (C)

PICTURES OF ELVIS
Return to sender: Roustabout: Little Egypt: Paradise Hawaiian style: Girls girls girls: Double trouble: Do the clam: Fun in Acapulco: Bossa nova baby: Clambake: Girl happy: Rock-a-hula baby
HY 1023 (LP) **TT** **HY8 1023** (S8) **TT**
HYK 1023 (C) **TT**

ELVIS (from the soundtrack of the NBC-TV SPECIAL)
Trouble: Guitar man: Lawdy, Miss Clawdy: Baby what you want me to do: Dialogue: Medley—Heartbreak Hotel—Hound dog—All shook up—Can't help falling in love—Jailhouse rock—Dialogue—Love me tender: Dialogue: Where could I go but to the Lord: Up above my head: Saved: Dialogue: Blue Christmas: Dialgoue: One night: Memories: Medley—Nothingville—Dialogue—Big boss man—Guitar man—Little Egypt—Trouble—Guitar man—If I can dream
(m)RD 8011 (LP) (LPM 4088)
P8S 1391 (S8) **VCS 67243** (C)

ELVIS
That's all right: Lawdy Miss Clawdy: Mystery train: Playing for keeps: Poor boy: Money honey: I'm counting on you: My baby left me: I was the one: Shake, rattle and roll: I'm left, you're right, she's gone: You're a heartbreaker: Tryin' to get to you: Blue suede shoes
PK 11529 (C)

ELVIS (ROCK 'N' ROLL No. 2)
Rip it up: Love me: When my blue moon turns to gold again: Long tall Sally: First in line: Paralysed: So glad you're mine: Old Shep: Ready Teddy: Any place is paradise: How's the world treating you: How do you think I feel (with *The Jordanaires)*
(s)SF 7528 (e) (LP) (LSP 1382 (e))
P8S 11530 (S8) **PK 11530** (C)

ELVIS—A LEGENDARY PERFORMER—VOL. 1
That's all right: I love you because: Heartbreak Hotel: Elvis (excerpt from an interview held September 22, 1958); Don't be cruel: Love me: Trying to get to you: Love me tender: (There'll be) Peace in the valley (for me) (with *The Jordanaires*): Elvis (further excerpt from an interview held September 22, 1958): (Now and then there's) A fool such as I (with *The Jordanaires*): Tonight is so right for love: Are you lonesome tonight: Can't help falling in love (with *The Jordanaires)*
(s)CPL1 0341 (LP) **HH**
(booklet insert with record)
APS1 0341 (S8) **SS** **APK1 0341** (C) **MM**

ELVIS as recorded live on stage in Memphis
See see rider: I got a woman: Love me: Trying to get to you: Medley—Long tall Sally/Whole lot-ta shakin' goin' on/Mama don't dance(Flip, flop and fly/Jailhouse rock/Hound dog: Why, Lord: How great Thou art: Medley—Blueberry Hill/I can't stop loving you: Help me: An American trilogy: Let me be there: My baby left me: Lawdy, Miss Clawdy: Can't help falling in love: Closing—vamp (with vocal accompaniment by *Voice, J. D. Sumner & The Stamps, The Sweet Inspirations, Kathy Westmoreland)*
(s)APL1 0606 (LP) **HH**
APS1 0606 (S8) **SS** **APK1 0606** (C) **MM**

ELVIS—A LEGENDARY PERFORMER—VOL. 2
Harbour lights: 1956 radio interview: I want you, I need you, I love you: Blue suede shoes: Blue Christmas: Jailhouse rock: It's now or never: A cane & a high starched collar: Pearl Harbour presentation: Blue Hawaii: Baby what do you want me to do: How great Thou art: If I can dream

ELVIS TODAY
T-r-o-u-b-l-e: And I love her so: Susan when she tried: Woman without love: Shake a hand: Pieces of my life: Fairytail: I can help: Bringing it back: Green green grass of home
RS 1011

ELVIS IN DEMAND
Suspicion: High heeled sneakers: Gotta lot o livin' to do: Have I told you lately that I love you: Please don't drag that string around: It's only love: The sound of your cry: Viva Las Vegas: Do not disturb: Tomorrow is a long time: It's a long lonely highway: Puppet on a string: First time ever I saw your face: Summer kisses, winter tears: It hurts me: Let it be me

ELVIS PRESLEY BOULEVARD
Hurt: Never again: Blue eyes crying in the rain:

Danny boy: The last farewell: For the heart: Bigger they are the harder they fall: Solitaire: Lovecoming down: I'll never fall in love again

RS 1060

POPULAR IMPORTED ALBUMS

IT HAPPENED AT THE WORLD'S FAIR
Beyond the bend: Relax: Take me to the fair: They remind me too much of you: One broken heart for sale: I'm falling in love tonight: Cotton candy lane: A world of our own: How would you like to be: Happy ending

RD 7565 (SF 7565)

HAREM HOLIDAY
Harem holiday: My desert serenade: Go east, young man: Mirage: Kismet: Shake that tambourine: Hey little girl: Golden coins: So close yet so far: Animal instinct: Wisdom of the ages

RD 7767 (SF 7767)

FRANKIE AND JOHNNY
Frankie and Johnny: Come along: Petunia: The gardener's daughter: Chesay: What every woman lives for: Look out, Broadway: Beginner's luck: Down by the riverside: When the saints go marching in: Shout it out: Hard luck: Please don't stop loving me: Everybody come aboard

RD 7792 (SF 7793)

PARADISE HAWAIIAN STYLE
Hawaii, USA: Queen Wahine's papaya: Scratch my back: Drums of the island: Datin': It's a dog's life: Castle made of sand: Stop where you are: This is my heaven: Sand castles

RD 7810 (SF 7810)

CALIFORNIA HOLIDAY
Stop, look and listen: Adam and evil: All that I am: Never say yes: Am I ready: Beach shack: Spinout: Smorgasbord: I'll be back: Tomorrow is a long time: Down in the alley: I'll remember you

RD 7820 (SF 7820)

DOUBLE TROUBLE
Double trouble: Baby, if you'll give me all of your love: Could I fall in love: Long-legged girl with the short dress on: City by night: Old Mac-Donald: I love only one girl: There is so much world to see: It won't be long: Never ending: Blue river: What now, what next, where to

RD 7892 (SF 7892)

CLAMBAKE
Guitar man: Who needs money: A house that has everything: Confidence: Hey, hey, hey: You don't know me: The girl I never loved: How can you lose what you never had: Big boss man: Singing tree: Just call me lonesome

RD 7917 (SF 7917)

SPEEDWAY
Speedway: There ain't nothing like a song: Your time hasn't come yet Baby: Who are you: He's your uncle not your dad: Let yourself go: Your groovy self: Five sleepy heads: Western union: Mine: Goin' home: Suppose: Nancy Sinatra only

RD 7957 (SF 7957)

ELVIS PRESLEY
Blue suede shoes: I'm counting on you: I got a woman: One-sided love affair: I love you because: Just because: Tutti frutti: Tryin' to get to you: I'm gonna sit right down and cry: I'll never let you go: Blue moon: Money honey

LSP 1254

LOVING YOU
Mean woman blues: Teddy bear: Loving you: Got a lot o' livin' to do: Lonesome cowboy: Hot dog: Party: Blueberry hill: True love: Don't leave me now: Have I told you lately that I love you: I need you so

LSP 1515

FOR LP FANS ONLY
That's all right: Lawdy, Miss Clawdy: Mystery train: Playing for keeps: Poor boy: My baby left me: I was the one: shake, rattle and roll: I'm left, you're right, she's gone: You're a heartbreaker

LSP 1990

ROUSTABOUT
Roustabout: Little Egypt: Poison ivy league: Hard knocks: It's a wonderful world: Big love: Big heart-ache: One track heart: It's carnival time: Carny town: There's a brand new day on the horizon: Wheels on my heels

LSP 2999

ELVIS FOR EVERYONE
Summer kisses—winter tears: Your cheatin' heart: Finders keepers, losers, weepers: For the millionth and the last time: Forget me never: I met her today: In my way: Memphis, Tennessee: Santa Lucia: Sound advice: Tomorrow night: When it rains it really pours

LSP 3450

A DATE WITH ELVIS
Blue moon of Kentucky: Young and beautiful: Baby I don't care: Milkcow blues boogie: Baby let's play house: Good rockin' tonight: Is it so strange: We're gonna move: I want to be free: I forgot to remember to forget

LSP 2011

POT LUCK WITH ELVIS
Kiss me quick: Just for old times sake: Gonna get back home somehow: Easy question: Steppin' out of line: I'm yours: Something blue: Suspicion: I feel that I've known you forever: Night rider: Fountain of love: That's someone you never forget

LSP 2523

GIRLS! GIRLS! GIRLS!
Girls! girls! girls!: Don't wanna be tied: Where do you come from: I don't want to: We'll be together: A boy like me, a girl like you: Earth boy: Return to sender: Because of love: Thanks to the rolling sea: Song of the shrimp: The walls have ears: We're coming in loaded

LSP 2621

FUN IN ACAPULCO
Fun in Acapulco: Vino, dinero y amor: Mexico el toro: Margarita: The bullfighter was a lady: There's no room to rhumba in a sports car: I think I'm gonna like it here: Bossa nova baby: You can't say no in Acapulco: Guadalajara: Love me tonight: Slowly but surely

LSP 2756

KISSIN' COUSINS
Kissin' cousins (number 2): Smokey mountain boy: There's gold in the mountains: One boy, two little girls: Catchin' on fast: Tender feeling: Anyone: Barefoot ballad: Once is enough: Kissin' cousins: Echoes of love: (It's a) long lonely highway

LSP 2894

GIRL HAPPY
Girl happy: Spring fever: Fort Lauderdale chamber of commerce: Wolf call: Startin' tonight: Do not disturb: Cross my heart: Meanest girl in town: Do the clam: I've got to find my baby: Puppet on a string: You'll be gone

LSP 3338

—CODES: LP Album; S8 Cartridge; C Cassette; Q Quadrophonic—
The catalogue is current as we go to press. However, an up-to-date list of Elvis' record releases (including many now-deleted albums) can be obtained by sending a s.a.e. to: Record Catalogue, Elvis Monthly, 41/43 Derby Road, Heanor, Derbyshire DE7 7QH.
—A price list will also be included—

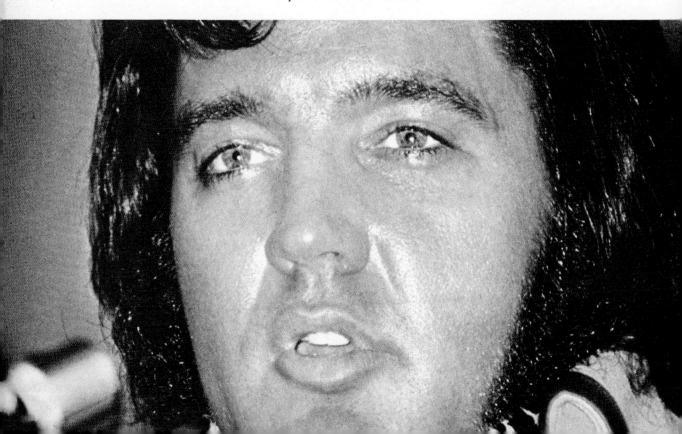

The Vintage Elvis Club

In last year's Annual I told you how I got involved with the fan club, plus the Vintage Club. This year I thought I would go into more detail about the club, its aims and its functions. Let me briefly explain how we first got started.

In 1968 I sold all my Elvis collection which at the time, I was told, was one of the best in Great Britain. Anyway, I sold it because I was offered an Elvis film to buy in 16mm sound, and as I could not afford it the only thing I could do was to sell my collection. I was very reluctant to do this but the temptation was too much, so as I say, I sold my Elvis collection and made a small fortune—and of course, bought the film, which was *Wild in the Country*. I then had to buy a projector which at that time cost me £180 (a lot of money for 1968)—and that projector is still going well today for you Elvis fans.

In 1969 I was offered three more films. These were *Flaming Star*, *Follow that Dream* and *Roustabout*— so you see the films were coming fast. The one I wanted most of all was *King Creole* and as luck would have it I got it, but just before this I was offered *Loving You*.

We now come to the events we have done up and down the country. We, the Vintage Club have entertained thousands of Elvis fans over the last seven years. The first time I rolled the projector for Elvis fans was in Leicester in 1970, when we had a get-together in a place called the "Fudidudi".

We had dancing plus movie, the movie was *Love in Las Vegas*, and I remember I was very scared to work the projector in case it broke down. Luck was with me, everything went very well and everyone had a great time, I'm very pleased to say.

A lot of water has gone under the bridge since that first event. Things were going very well and as some of the films we had were no longer on the cinema rounds due to the rights being taken away, we thought we would do a film show—the first major film show we did—again in Leicester. This was in November '71 and was attended by a good number of fans.

In 1972 we went on tour, and in February we did an event for Peter Wilson in London. How I remember this one, as I was on the night shift at the time. I finished nights at six in the morning and, feeling very tired, drove all the way to London and showed seven

Elvis films which were *King Creole*, *Follow that Dream*, *Loving You*, *Wild in the Country*, *Blue Hawaii*, *Roustabout* and *Love me Tender*. I was so glad to see the last one go into the projector!

About a week after this event I received a telegram from the States to inform me that *Elvis—That's the Way it is* was up for sale—so I sent for it. Again this film cost a small fortune, but I think this is the best Elvis film made. We then had an event in Bury, which again went down very well. The following month we had an event in Coventry, and about a week before this *Elvis—That's the Way it is* came. The problem about getting films from the States is that you have to pay customs duty on them and to date the club has paid between £200 and £300 in Customs alone.

Back to the story. I was able to take our new movie with me to Coventry, and the fans enjoyed it so much I had to put the last reel on again. In that year, 1972, we visited no less than 11 cities. From the proceeds we were able to buy a second projector, plus some more movies for the film library.

Since '72 we have been to many areas to entertain the Elvis fans and our film library has grown to 14 Elvis films, as well as clips, newsreels, and TV shows. Some of the cream of the collection consists of such greats as *Change of Habit*, *Aloha from Hawaii*, *Elvis—That's the Way it is*, *Love me Tender* and *Ed Sullivan TV Shows*. The club has also gone into Video, and by having this we are able to show just about anything on Elvis. We have possibly the best Elvis film library in the World.

Since 1972 we have entertained Elvis fans overseas in Norway, Germany, France, Belgium, Holland and Luxembourg. At the beginning of 1976 we introduced the Major Bailye disco to the events, which is proving a great success. These events are great because they give fans more time to get to know each other and at the same time they have such a great time dancing to the music of Elvis. I really enjoy these events, where we also have a bar, giving more atmosphere.

Well, that's given you more of an insight into the film side of the club. We entertain you in the shape of films and disco, and we always have a Vintage Elvis stall where you can buy Elvis items.

Now to tell you about the other side of the club which is the products side. We try to obtain early items for collectors, books, records, in fact just about anything on Elvis, and we are also producing exclusive souvenirs such as T-shirts, stickers, dusters, badges, and lots of new items are being introduced all the time to add to the vast range which we already have. So if you have not had a catalogue yet, I suggest you write today and find out what you are missing in your Elvis collection.

We also operate a swop and sell with the club. If you have something to sell, we buy it at a fair price. We also swop anything on Elvis, so as you can see, this is how the Vintage Club operates to make money to buy new movies, and to pay for the upkeep of all the equipment—the Video, projectors etc.

So, till the next time stay 100% for Elvis and support your fan club. If you require a catalogue from the Vintage Club write to Ian R. Bailye, Graceland, Equity Rd, Earl Shilton, Leicester LE9 7FD, England.

IAN BAILYE

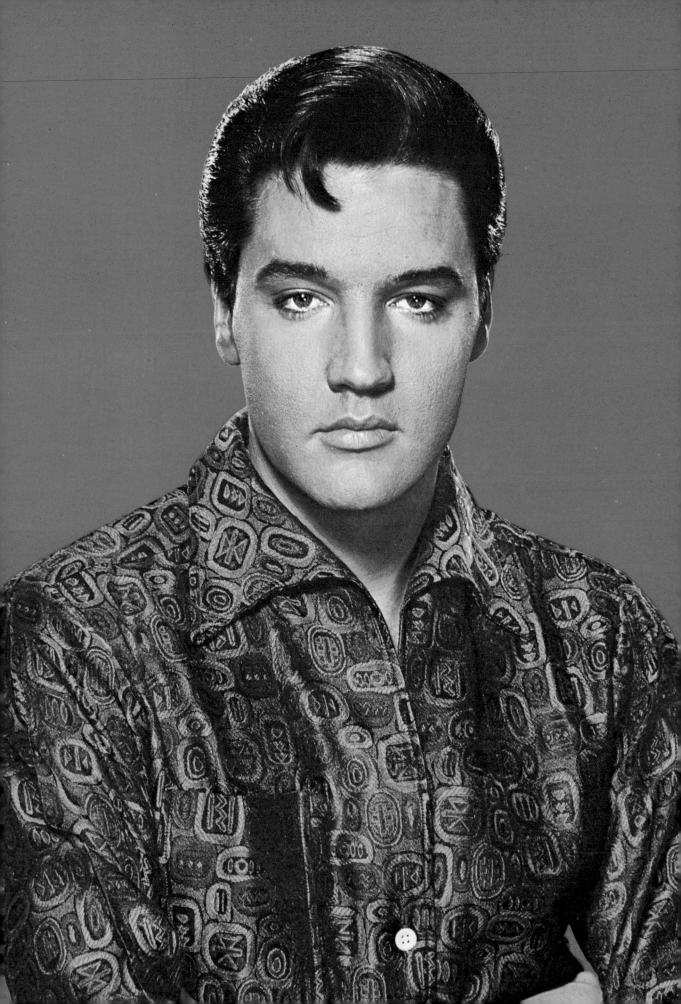

Will Elvis Progress – or Stagnate with Rock?

by R. Nokes

In the Elvis Special 1977 I posed the question, "Will pop music ever be respected as a serious music form?" and concluded my article by saying this would never be. So in this article I would like to examine what will be the direction of pop/rock music during the next few years, with emphasis on Elvis' contribution or non-contribution in this period.

It is almost certain that the "pop culture" will be aimed at the very young, and will continue to take the place of the comics etc which used to be aimed at this particular age group. The utterly tasteless drivel of this type of music will no doubt continue as long as we have "lively Radio One" and people like Tony Blackburn who are overjoyed to play *Remember you're a Womble* several times a week. Alright, I know we need MOR music for those who enjoy it, but why do the minority musical groups have to suffer as a result? Still, that's another question altogether which maybe I'll go into one day.

Elvis, I hope, will steer clear of the "pop" culture field as he really doesn't need to record or be recognised with this type of music. Recent "pop" recordings by Elvis such as *Take Good Care of Her* and *She Wears my Ring* make me want to re-examine all the views I hold and believe in Presley's musical awareness. In the book "Elvis" by Jerry Hopkins, Scotty Moore is quoted as saying of Elvis, "I don't think even today he realises what he's done." If this is true it would answer the question of why Elvis shows no sense of responsibility in either his recordings or film career. I know in the last few years Elvis has been unwell, but this state of affairs has nearly always been in existence since 1962.

So while "pop" will almost certainly become more stereotyped during the next few years, I can only hope that Elvis stops and rethinks his attitude to this type of music. Or perhaps it will be the case of follow the trend instead of creating a good solid music reputation which has, and let's be quite honest, taken some hard knocks during Elvis' career.

The progression of rock music, however, may well reach new heights in the next few years. *Jesus Christ Superstar* and *Joseph* by Rice and Lloyd-Webber have rock music in their interpretation of biblical stories. The success of these shows that rock music can appeal to the majority, both young and old, and it needn't

be "watered down" for mass acceptance by the public. Rice and Lloyd-Webber are both very pro-Elvis, witness only the character of Pharaoh in *Joseph* if you doubt my word. And it does seem a shame that nothing has ever happened between these three, although that's what I've said about Elvis and Phil Spector and Lennon, etc, etc, etc—makes you weep doesn't it. Here we have the greatest rock interpreter ever and all we can get in the last few years is about one album's worth of good creative recordings.

One hard fact cannot be denied by any fan who is honest with himself, and that is that Elvis is scared of change in his career. He hasn't much confidence in himself for new projects, this is why we always get too much of everything, witness films, live albums, touring America till he makes himself ill. All these things in excess instead of changing to something new every now and again. The no-confidence factor is why he is very rarely produced by really good producers,

because if he set himself a really high standard in recordings he would be scared he could not keep up the standard set. If you think that's rubbish, dig out your old Elvis clippings and read what Elvis said about his film career when he reached the age of 30. "I realise I must never bite off more than I can chew. . . . If I made an art picture and it clicked I'd be scared I couldn't repeat it." Insecurity in his own ability I'd say, still, each to his own opinion.

Still, I digress from the subject. With rock music's progression, thanks first to the Beatles and lately to groups like the Moody Blues and Santana, a new era has been entered. The fusion of different types of music has been attempted and succeeded (witness Santana's latin/rock musical fusion, and the Moodies' rock/symphony offerings). The potential of this type of musical integration is limitless, and the possibilities exciting and endless. Who, ten years ago, would have thought that Deep Purple would perform at the Albert Hall with a top symphony orchestra? The fusion of these different types of music is to be applauded, because it will eventually break down the barriers of musical snobbery which have prevailed for many years.

Elvis, I fear, will make no contribution in this field as he is "limited" in his present musical outlook and also because I don't think he will try anything that's different at this stage in his career. However, what a thought, if we had Elvis, Eric Clapton, Rick Wakeman and say Buddy Rich on one album, backed by the London Symphony Orchestra. This fusion of the various musical styles might not work, but if it did (as in Bangla Desh album) what a giant of an album it would turn out to be! Although recording contracts might interfere, if each company was allowed to retail the subsequent album the venture would easily pay for itself.

So, you might say, where do I think Elvis will be, musically, in a few years time? What, if I believe that (A) he should steer clear of "pop" and (B) he will not progress with the "rock culture", do I think he will be doing? Unless I am mistaken I believe he will continue in his present vein: Vegas, occasional LPs, singles etc.

However, I will predict that if one Colonel Parker is replaced by someone young with modern ideas of management of a star, then Elvis Presley will again lead rock instead of trying to be all things to all people musically, which never works. Remember, this article is being written at the end of 1976, so let's hope that by Christmas 1977 the only Colonel Tom in the rock field is the one in Bowie's musical output, although of course he is a "Major Tom". Still, with records such as *Elvis in Memphis* there must be hope, don't you agree?

The Role of the Critic ~ KAY PARLEY

Perhaps one should approach the subject of criticism through the eyes of those who are most concerned, the creative artists themselves. To begin with, there are four stages to the creative process:

Stage one, *Preparation*, consists of gathering information, facts, experiences, knowledge, or whatever will provide raw material and technique for the job of creation.

Stage two, *Incubation*, is the stage in which this material is put away into the subconscious mind to "process", a stage of quiescence when the conscious mind shuts off and the ideas are left to simmer. During this stage the mind seems to automatically form new associations and prepare the creative organisation.

Stage three, *Inspiration*, is the actual creative stage, when the artist usually feels a great upsurge of energy and joy, often touching upon euphoria, and when he rides the crest of this energy and creates his product. Inventive geniuses make their scientific inventions during this period, writers write their books, painters produce their pictures, composers write their music. Even creative mathematicians have analysed the stages of creativity in this way.

But there is always a fourth stage. Mathematicians call it *Verification* and psychologists call it *Validation*. Artists call it a lot of names and never enjoy it much. It is the critical phase. The bright glory of stage three disappears and leaves in its wake a cold, critical, rational frame of mind, often bereft of all the love for the product which the artist so recently knew. The writer reads over his book and hates it; the painter finds a hundred errors in his painting. Some artists train themselves to keep a critical view turned on throughout most of the creative process.

In *Music and Imagination*, Aaron Copland wrote, "The creative mind, in its day-to-day functioning, must be critical mind." He went on to add that self-critical appraisal of the composer's own mind guiding the composition to completion was particularly difficult, for, as he put it, "Music is an emotional and comparatively intangible substance." Perhaps it is easier to play the self-critic when one is writing or painting.

Why, if it is such an unpleasant task, do creative artists use the critical faculty at all? Why do writers discard entire novels? Painters junk hundreds of sketches? Singers destroy their tapes rather than have them reach a platter?

The answer is simple, and it was said many years ago, in a familiar old proverb: "Build a better mouse-trap and the world will beat a path to your door". Unfortunately, if you build an inferior mousetrap the world will not beat any path at all. They may ignore you or, worse, they may laugh at you. That is the bitter truth about creativity. A scientific invention must be useful and operative or it will be scorned. The art product must have something to say to the public or they will reject it.

Of recent years there has been a trend toward viewing creativity as a fun process, a means of self-expression, and viewed in this way it allows one to disregard the critical phase.

Art is valid as long as the artist himself is getting something out of it. It doesn't have to please anyone else. It was a mistaken philosophy for, as time will reveal, only those works which have meaning will survive. Criticism is built right into the creative process because the creative process has no validity until it is tested by the public. This is a social reality and it has been reality since man discovered fire and the wheel.

Well then, if artists have the ability to do their own criticism and reject their own failures, hopefully before they are shown to the public, why do we need professional critics? Why do newspapers and maga-zines pay writers whose only job is to see movies or read books or listen to records and write reviews of them?

There are at least three reasons: To begin with there is always the possibility that the artist failed to criticise his own work satisfactorily. Many an artist cannot bring himself to reject his brain children, even if they are not up to standard. Secondly, especially in this technological age, the product may be out of the hands of the artist himself. The publisher or the recording company may be pushing the work even though it is a bad piece of "creativity". The critic is supposed to protect the public from poor material, and that brings me to the third reason for critics—they save you and I time, money, and frustration.

If I read a book review and the critic tells me that it is poor or if he tells me that it contains information that doesn't interest me, I won't buy it. I have either to trust the critic or buy the book, and with the millions of books being published these days it is a lot easier to trust the critic. The same goes for other things. I haven't time to go to all the movies and listen to all the records. But there is somebody in society with a very useful role—the guy whose job it is to see the movies and listen to the records for me. He can save me a lot of money.

Of course I am critical myself, and I make sure that the critics I read are in reputable magazines, so I am an avid reader of *Harper's* and *Saturday Review*, where some of the most intelligent critics can be found. Elvis is the only artist I will buy without reading the critical reviews, and that is because Elvis, as far as I'm concerned, is special. I love the man! I'll buy anything he sings.

Still another function of the critic emerges. For instance I will eagerly read any good critical review of an Elvis movie or an Elvis album. Why, when I've already seen it or bought it? Because at least 50% of the fun of appreciation is finding out how others have reacted. If the critic likes something I like I can pat myself on the back with glee and say, "See? He's a professional and I am as smart as he is! I saw the same thing!"

If the critic disagrees with me it helps me to define my own position, to re-evaluate and perhaps to change my mind. At least it will urge me to reconsider my reasons and it will put my own sense of appreciation on a firmer footing.

Half of the intellectual game of theatre-going is to discuss the play with friends later, and then to discuss what the critics said. Theatre critics have tremendous power, especially in the United States. In *Change Lobsters and Dance*, Lilli Palmer writes that when Broadway reigned supreme the critic functioned as, "a sort of taster to the eight million inhabitants of New York City." If he liked the play the line formed at the box office. If he didn't, you were dead. Critics of the *Times* and *Tribune* could break a production over-night, "just as the Roman emperors could determine by a movement of the thumb whether a gladiator was to live or die."

Critics are the bane of many an actor, writer, painter, or singer, but God love them they also stimulate so much interest and controversy that many a famous man would never have been heard of without them. Remember, those 1954 critics who panned Elvis brought him as much (or more) atten-tion as those who praised!

Critics are human. They make mistakes, and they suffer from a peculiar brand of cynicism and ennui. Imagine having to appraise plays, or books, or art exhibits, or recordings, day after day, year after year, decade after decade. It must be a tedious job and it must make one hate the world at times. What's more, critics are paid to be critical. As Parker Tyler states in *Magic and Myth of the Movies* (Simon and Schuster, 1947), "this mercenary habit has rendered the critic's finer sensibilities a little warped and petulant, not to say also vicious and abnormal." Strong words, but we must remember that the critic's profession forces him to suffer through it all, good and bad. It is his job to judge trends and tastes and to know what the public will accept, and he often does his job well.

So far I haven't published any books for the critics to review, but I have shown a few paintings and directed a few plays, and I know the thrill of finding rave reviews in the newspaper and the alternate chill of finding lukewarm to cold reviews. The artist and the critic are in a game together. The artist makes the moves; the critic, by checking and prodding and evaluating, helps to protect the public, stimulate the public, and at the same time encourage the artist to do better and better. Creative fields might be terribly dull without him.

We have an art critic here in Saskatoon, Saskatchewan, whom I dislike. I've never met her, but I know I don't like her, because she consistently raves over paintings I hate and turns a cold shoulder to any exhibition I like. We recently had a show of Canadian painters of the 1930s and she called it obscure and said it was impossible to intuit herself into the art of such a long-ago age. I thought the show was great!

Which illustrates another important point about critics and criticism: you can't trust all of the critics all of the time, and serious students of any branch of the arts learn which critic is which. There is a movie critic I like very much and I trust what he says. If he says a film is one of the best of the year, I'll go see it. But when it comes to our local art critic I will never go to a show because she says it's good or avoid it simply because she says it's bad. It is up to me to find out about her and to pit my own judgments against hers. Yet I read her reviews almost every week. She stimulates my interest, and that in itself is important.

It goes without saying, I think, that a critic is expected to have reasons for his judgments, and a good critic will let the public know his reasons. He is not there to force his opinions down resistant throats. He is there to evaluate and to provide valid reasons for his evaluations. He should make us think and look and listen and get more out of the creative arts.

I think that a misunderstanding of what critical judgment is all about lies at the root of some of the controversy that keeps arising in Elvis fandom over this issue. For example, in one issue of *The Strictly Elvis Generation*, Scott Stumpf revived this all-too-familiar theme with the statement, "Judgment is neither ours nor the critics' right." Scott is absolutely wrong. Judgment is everybody's right. Along with reasoning, planning, conceptualising, abstracting, imagining, remembering, deciding, inventing, criticising, designing, and creating, it is one of the things which man can do with his highest faculty—the faculty of reason. A fat lot of fools we would be with-

out it. Judging is not only our right, it is our bounden duty as human beings.

If, on the other hand, Scott means by "critic" someone who attacks Elvis as a personality, gossips about his private life, or in any way says things which would be better unsaid, then I sympathise. But this isn't criticism; this is *attack*. Criticism should be constructive. It is an old truism in group dynamics, known to all T-group and sensitivity training groups, that the fellow who feels the need to pick on or belittle or verbally attack another member of the group is really the one with the problem. It isn't the fellow being picked on who has the problem. He is merely being used as a sounding board.

Anyone who reacts to this kind of attack by taking it personally or by feeling that Elvis will take it personally is allowing himself to be dragged into the game. The issue is not whether the slander is true or whether it is hurting Elvis. The only pertinent issue is why does the attacker feel the need to attack? Is it hidden jealousy? Does the cut of Elvis' hair remind him of someone he doesn't much like? Does something in Elvis' personality remind him of something he doesn't really accept and admire in his own personality? And what does it matter anyway? What on earth does it have to do with Elvis? The attacker could just as easily pick on someone else to attack.

The critic, on the other hand, has a legitimate, recognised role in our society. Sometimes he may madden us and annoy us, but we do him a great disservice when we confuse his role with some misguided soul with a psychological quirk which makes him want to attack. In the role of critic a person has the right to disagree, to dislike, even to despise, and as long as he has a reason for his reaction he is not attacking, he is criticising. There is a world of difference between the two, and though *Elvis Monthly* has a few attackers (they attack the critics, not Elvis!), we also have a number of excellent critics who understand the role and play it well. Long may they reign!

ELVISTEIN —
— MAN OR MONSTER
by Terry Mailey Jnr.

Come friends and listen to this tale that I am about to unfold. If you be of faint heart then read no further. For those of you that do wish to hear my tale, be warned, there are incidents that are not suitable for the ears of children, nor the eyes of women, so keep this edition of the "Elvis Special" safely out of their reach. Now read on if you will.

It was a cold winter in '55 and Professor Parker, the eminent surgeon of Tennessee University, was about to unleash a "being" upon the population of America; one that would wreak havoc wherever he went. This being he called Elvis.

This Elvis was a super-being made up from various parts of other celebrities. He had the body of Rock Hudson, famous beefcake star of Universal movies. Professor Parker had secured his body and replaced it with a robot that was so life-like that nobody knew that he was really an automaton. Some critics, however, may have guessed, as they said his acting was rather animated.

The head of this Elvis being was that of a Greek God whose body had recently been excavated from ruins in Greece. The body, which was countless centuries old, had decayed, but the head was miraculously still young and had been preserved by some magic known only to the ancient Greeks.

The head and body of this Elvis being had been secured for Professor Parker by his deformed assistant, Ygor, who had also secured the voice for the being, a voice which he had stolen from the "Country Hall of Fame" in nearby Nashville, Tennessee.

The Professor had spent countless months assembling his creation, this Elvis being, and on that storm-filled evening of two decades ago he brought it to life by injecting music into the bloodstream and soul into the heart. The being that was Elvis rose from the operating table and, facing the Professor, it mumbled, "Hi, this is Elvis Presley."

"You fool, Ygor," the Professor shouted, "whose voice did you steal? Marlon Brando's?"

Before Ygor could answer, the being called Elvis spied a guitar in the operating theatre and began to play it and sing in a strange yet haunting voice.

"Ygor," the Professor cried, "your blunder could have been a brainwave."

Ygor looked at his master, unable to grasp what he meant.

"Why," the Professor said, "this being, with his good looks, unusual singing voice and strange-sounding name could be 'monstrous' in the entertainment world!"

Ygor grunted in agreement and rolled his eyes in best Peter Lorre fashion.

The Professor, who had connections in the showbiz world, got his Elvis creature a booking on the *Ed Sullivan TV Show* for January of 1956.

That fateful night the monster was unleashed onto the unsuspecting American public. The minute the "beat" music started the creature became uncontrollable and began to gyrate all over the place. The Professor all but tore out his hair.

"Ygor, you fool," he ranted. "I'm ruined!"

The TV companies banned the being called Elvis from appearing before their cameras again. However, public demand was so great to see the monster again that Ed Sullivan relented and agreed to have the Professor's creation appear again.

In an effort to stop a repeat happening of Elvis' first performance, Ed Sullivan had the creature chained to a spot and filmed from the waist up, so that the TV audience couldn't see the restricting bonds. However, like King Kong, Elvis broke his bonds and went into a full frenzy once the "beat" music began.

After this second TV appearance the Professor took his creation out on the road, and had it perform its hideous act in theatres all over the United States. Wherever the Elvis being appeared, whole groups of teenagers would riot and the poor creature was blamed for the furore that ensued. Then—like in those old science-fiction movies—the army was called in to help save the country from this alien being, Elvis.

Elvis was caught and held captive for two years, being shipped to Germany for part of the time. His lengthy hair was cut short, G.I. fashion, and like Samson in the Bible his strength was sapped.

Upon his release from the army, it was clear to the world that the beast had been tamed. For the next

decade the creature was sent to a detention camp called "Hollywood" and it was thought by the world at large that the Elvis being had died there.

However, there were a legion of people called "fans" who had sympathy, and indeed admiration for the Elvis being and they beseeched his creator, Professor Parker, to unleash his creation upon the world once more. The Professor, touched by this feeling, took his Elvis being out of Hollywood and into the deserts of Nevada to a town called Las Vegas, and there he let him rant and rave for his "fans". The monster of the fifties was now happy and twice yearly he went on the rampage in the Hilton Hotel, just to let the world know that he was still a force to be reckoned with.

And to this day, and perhaps until time immemorial he will continue to do his "thing" there for his legion of "fans", the people who had set him free from his exile, for there's an old saying "Old monsters never die—they just haunt you forever".

Elvis & The Early Media by TONY NEALE

There have been several articles in the monthly touching on Elvis' Stateside television appearances, but I thought it would be interesting to do a more comprehensive study of these early broadcasts, and try to build up a clear picture of just what Elvis was like on stage in those very early days, so here goes:

Elvis was unleashed for the first time on a startled nationwide audience via the Jackie Gleason/Dorsey Brothers show on 28 January 1956. Cleveland disc jockey Bill Randall introduced him on the show, saying amongst other things that he thought Elvis would make television history that night—how right he was.

For his debut Elvis performed *Shake, Rattle and Roll*, which at the time he had yet to put on disc; this live version was a strange hybrid, borrowing lyrics from both the Bill Haley and Joe Turner versions, and finishing up with a verse from Turner's *Flip, Flop and Fly*. "Ahm like a Mississippi bullfrog sittin' on a hollow stump," sang the young Elvis, licking his lips and rolling his eyes, "ah got so many women, ah don't know which way to jump." Judging from still photos taken from this initial appearance, Elvis had no difficulty in jumping around at all, alternately hugging the microphone and dancing way back near Scotty, Bill and D. J. Fontana during the instrumental breaks, with the studio lights bouncing off his dark suit and coal-black shirt.

Elvis' second number was *I Got a Woman*, which he had cut just two weeks earlier, and the live version follows the studio one pretty faithfully.

It's interesting to note here the reaction of the studio audience to this initial Presley appearance; there were no screams as yet, but during the instrumental breaks when, presumably, Elvis is leaping around the stage, there is a lot of shouting and cheering with a huge round of applause at the end of the songs. Even on sound only, all these years later the atmosphere is electric whilst Elvis is on stage, transmitting all that energy outwards in great shock-waves.

Elvis appeared on six Gleason shows altogether and, while I haven't heard all of the numbers he did, I've heard most and I'll comment on these now.

He did *Money Honey*, *I Was the One* and *Blue Suede Shoes* a couple of times, and several others only once.

To my surprise, the debut version of *Heartbreak Hotel* features a low-down dixieland backing similar to the *King Creole* tracks, rather than guitar and bass. I guess that the idea of opening the '68 TV special with *Trouble* was because of its similarity to the TV debut of *Hotel*, but Elvis didn't seem too happy with the jazzy back-up, which seemed to mess-up his timing somewhat and sounded like a failed attempt to temper his fiery country-blues sound with a jazzy, urban sophistication. However, the next time he did it, the regular backing was used and it sounded immeasurably better.

The version of *Blue Suede Shoes* I've heard is basically a cross between Carl Perkins' and Elvis' own version, taken a bit slower than the recorded cut.

The two best Gleason numbers I've heard are *Baby Let's Play House* and *Tutti Frutti*. *House* was the only Sun track Elvis featured on the show, and he sings it in much the same way as on the record although, sad to say, you can hardly hear Scotty's guitar twanging away in the background.

Tutti Frutti had Elvis in great form even though, once again, Scotty was hardly audible. Elvis introduced the number thus: "And now a little song that really tells the story; it makes lotsa' sense . . . it goes somethin' like this. . . ." He later reserved this heavily-sarcastic introduction for *Hound Dog*.

Anyhow, *Tutti Frutti* really scorches along with (if that's possible) even more attack than the recorded version, and by this time Elvis was starting to get the screams which later accompanied his every move.

One other thing you notice from these early performances is the way that Elvis urges Scotty, Bill and D. J. on, pushing them all the time, shouting out encouragement and turning around to face them during the guitar breaks; it really adds a lot to the overall excitement.

I opened this article by saying this would be a "more comprehensive" look at those first TV appearances, but I must say I've never heard anything that Elvis did on his next TV date—namely the *Milton Berle Show*. I know he did a couple of shows, and I've seen stills of Elvis in action on them (and fantastic they look too), but I regret I haven't heard one note from them, nor do I know of anyone who has.

However, the next TV appearance, on the *Steve Allen Show*, presents no such problems. This was the one where they had Elvis dressed up in white tie and tails in an attempt to make his image more "respectable" and I must say, as Allen himself pointed out in the show, Elvis took this attempt to make him look foolish very well, participating in the light-hearted banter served up by Allen during his introduction. Before bringing Elvis onstage, Allen mentions the fuss created by his appearance on the Berle show a few weeks earlier and, because his is a family show, promises to reveal for the first time "the new Elvis Presley". Elvis comes on wearing the dress-suit but reveals he's also wearing something which might not be suitable for evening-wear, namely blue suede shoes! Then, after being presented with a "giant petition" signed by 18,000 loyal fans asking to see him on TV again, Elvis sings the first of his two songs: *I Want You, I Need You, I Love You*. This live version of the then-current US Presley hit is unremarkable, being weaker than either of the recorded versions, and nearer the recently-issued alternate take in delivery.

After this first number, Allen announces that Elvis will cut a new song the next day for his forthcoming new single, and then, singing to a real-live dog perched on a pedestal, Elvis launches into *Hound Dog*.

I was very curious to know what Elvis would do with this song before I got to hear it; would it be like the single, or would it be totally different?

The answer is neither one nor the other: the Allen live version is influenced by both the original recording via Willie Mae Thornton, and a copycat song cut by Rufus Thomas for Sun called *Bear Cat*; the rhythm is much looser and less intense than on the studio cut, without the piledriving chords of Scotty Moore urging it along. The live performance also has Elvis employing a stutter eg: "You ain't nothin' but a hound dog, c-cryin' all the time," which seems to be a little touch he invented himself.

The electric atmosphere featured on the Gleason shows is missing from the Allen broadcast, due probably to the way Elvis' performance was toned-down by the TV bosses, but despite everything, Elvis manages to come through it all with his persona intact. However, it makes you wonder just what Elvis did on the Milton Berle show to provoke the silliness demonstrated on the Allen programme.

Two months later, after swearing that Presley would never get onto his show, Ed Sullivan took a look at the ratings for the Allen show and paid out a record 50,000 dollars for him to do just that.

Elvis did three Sullivan shows altogether, the first of which took place on 9 September 1956. On that show, Elvis opened with *Don't Be Cruel* which, along with *Hound Dog*, was the number one record at the time. After this, he introduced the new single *Love Me Tender* for the first time, singing it to an accompaniment of "oohs" and "aahs" from the girls in the audience. Next came *Ready Teddy*, and we all know about that one don't we? A fabulous, dynamic rocking performance from Elvis, showcased so beautifully in the *Elvis On Tour* movie. If you saw Elvis perform it in that film, then you'll know that words are useless to describe it. After this song, Elvis sends a get-well message to Ed Sullivan, who was ill at the time, and proceeds to belt out a short, sharp version of *Hound Dog* to round off his contribution.

The next appearance was on 28 October 1956, when Elvis once again opened the proceedings with *Don't Be Cruel*—which was still the number one seller in the States. The pattern of the previous show continued further with *Love Me Tender* coming next; this time out, Elvis was in playful mood and played to the gallery, teasing the audience by slurring his words in places, eg: "For my darling I lllove you, and I always will." He also changed the words of one verse, singing, "Love me tender, love me when, we are far apart; I'll be with you even then, deep within your heart." Then, says Elvis, "Friends, we'd like to do a new song from the new album," and it's *Love Me*, with Elvis hamming it up unmercifully, laying on the heavy breathing with a trowel and clowning around with the lyrics, sending the girls in the audience into hysterics. At the finish of the song, Elvis pleads, "Please, please love me," runs his hands through that long greasy hair in mock anguish and disappears into the wings at a run, with the screams from the audience echoing in his ears. "Don't worry," says Ed Sullivan, "he's gonna be right back."

And boy, does Elvis come back! The final number proves to be a solid blockbuster! Elvis, resplendent in green jacket, black trousers and white suede shoes moves to centre-stage, gazes out into a sea of faces and says, "Ladies and gentlemen, I'd like to say that we're gonna do a . . . sad song for ya. This here's one of the saddest songs you've ever heard. Beautiful lyrics . . . it goes somethin' like this. . . ."

It's the same ploy he used to introduce *Tutti Frutti* back on the Gleason show, but the girls in the balcony aren't fooled for a minute. As Scotty strikes a bluesy chord, some of them yell out, "*Hound Dog*!" and,

sure enough, that's just what it is: a rockin', jumping no holds barred version which brings the house down. Even in those early days, Elvis was apt to fool around a lot on stage, teasing the crowd and sending himself up remorselessly; but there were times when a strange look would come into his eyes, or an urgency into his voice, some strange almost bitter attitude which made the hairs on your neck stand to attention.

It happened with *Ready Teddy* from the 9 September show, and it happens again on this second Sullivan date, with *Hound Dog*. Elvis really storms through the number without any let-up, bellowing out the beautiful lyrics through a literally non-stop barrage of piercing screams. It really is incredibly exciting, almost frightening, to hear the reception Elvis gets with this song. At the end of the number the screams are deafening, but a somewhat breathless Elvis manages to finally make himself heard: "Ladies and gentlemen, ah, I'd like to tell you friends, on Thanksgiving Day I think that our new picture is to be released and ah, also we'll be back with Mr. Ed Sullivan in January. I'd like to thank all the millions of wonderful people who are watching tonight, friends; and, ah, I'd like to say this, until we meet you again—may God bless you, as he's blessed me."

Elvis, true to his word, came back for his third and final appearance on the Sullivan show in January of '57, on the 6th to be exact. This time out, they had Elvis performing on a giant record with a backdrop of musical notes, and very impressive it looked too.

This time, by way of a change, Elvis opened with a shortened version of *Hound Dog*, followed by the usual *Love Me Tender*. Then, for the first time with Sullivan's show, he sang *Heartbreak Hotel*, a very bluesy but much condensed version which had the girls screaming as Elvis pretended to sob on the line, "Broken hearted lovers". "Thank you very much, ladies and gentlemen," says Elvis, "I'd like to do the song that was my very biggest record last year . . . I mean it was no bigger than the rest of them, but it sold a few more . . . and it goes like this," . . . and on into *Don't Be Cruel*. On this number, Elvis did something he'd done on the previous versions, that is, when he came to that "MMMMMmmm" bit in the song he'd exaggerate it madly, and then chuckle at the ecstatic response it received from the studio audience. However, unlike the other versions, right at the end of the number, after turning to Scotty, Bill, D. J. and the Jordanaires to whisper, "Here we go," he gave the song a big finish, his voice leaping an octave or so amid a barrage of screams from the audience.

At the time of going on the air, Elvis' brand new single was *Too Much* and he sang this next in much the same way as on the recorded version.

After this, Elvis told everyone he'd received,

"Exactly 282 teddy bears," during the Christmas holidays, and he wished he could buy every fan a new Lincoln car. Then, "Something from my album, fans," and into *When My Blue Moon Turns to Gold*, again, very similar to the recorded version.

For his final song, Elvis landed a surprise on the millions watching by performing *Peace in the Valley*, the first time he'd sung a sacred number on TV; in fact, he hadn't even recorded the song at that time (it was cut on 13 January 1957) and, despite a few dissenting voices who piously claimed that an "obscene" rock 'n' roller like Presley shouldn't be singing a religious song, it was largely due to the demand of his fans that Elvis recorded the number, along with a few other sacred tracks, the following week. Elvis' treatment of the song live is virtually identical to the recorded version, if much less dramatic, and it was to be the last number he sang on American television for over four years, until the Sinatra special of 12 May 1960.

So that's about the end of this look at Elvis on television during the mid-fifties. If, as has been suggested, he toned-down his act somewhat on these broadcasts, then his actual stage-act on one-nighters must have been really incredible. Both *Ready Teddy*, and the 28 October 1956 version of *Hound Dog* are dynamite performances, even on TV, so we get some idea of just what the 21-year-old Presley was capable of when the mood took him.

One other thing you notice from these shows is that, even in those early days, Elvis delighted in sending up both himself and his audience to a large extent, never really taking it all too seriously; an ability to get everything in perspective which has helped him to sail through the last 20 years virtually unscathed.

Someone should gather together film of all those fifties TV appearances and put them in a full-length movie so that everyone can see muscial history in the making for themselves; that clip of the young Elvis belting out *Ready Teddy* in the *On Tour* movie was a fine appetiser, now let's have the main course.

THE ELVIS EXPERIENCE
by NADINE RIGHTMYER

After seeing Elvis in person in Buffalo, N.Y. I'll never be the same again. I was very fortunate in seeing this show and got to see Elvis up close. After seeing him so close and hearing him perform several of my favourite songs with his BETTER THAN EVER voice in person—my desire to see him again is tremendous!

I met several of "Elvis' boys" at the Hilton Hotel for my first time, before and after the show. They are so nice and friendly. When I talked with James Burton and got his autograph I just had to ask him, "Doesn't the loud music make you deaf?" He leaned over close to me and said, "What?"

I can't help but say Elvis has passed the state of being gorgeous. His looks simply devastated me. Seeing him up that close. . . .

He was in a BEAUTIFUL mood, seemed so happy and really enjoyed everything he did.

His beautiful hair is long and such a deep black. He has just a *little* tummy, otherwise he's in terrific shape.

Elvis no sooner arrived on stage and began singing when some girl came running right at him. She gave him a bear hug and kisses. This time a girl had *HIM* all shook up—and he broke out laughing.

When he sang *Amen* he asked the audience to, "Sing it with me." Needless to say, almost every person in the place immediately began singing *Amen* and were also clapping enthusiastically.

He said, "I get very nervous on opening night, really."

The music was so loud and with the constant explosion of flashes, especially whenever he turned around to the back balcony—all I could think was, "Elvis' poor ears and eyes."

His beautiful versions of such songs as *And I Love You So*, *Love Letters*, *Early Morning Rain* and *Polk Salad Annie* brought forth a sea of sighs and endless moans and groans. He did a doubleleg split, slowly going down on one leg and then the other! (How does he do that?) He prefaced it by looking up at heaven and saying, "God help me."

Whenever he was holding a glass of water he would tease his fans by pretending he was going to throw it on them. His captivating smile showed he got a big kick out of teasing them.

When the house lights came on Elvis said, "Two hundred miles for a birthday kiss—c'mere sweetheart." El asked her what her name was and then he knelt down and sang *Happy Birthday* to her. When he kissed her the girl didn't want Elvis to leave, but he said, "No more." *Hail Rock 'n' Roll* was sung by El during the introductions.

When he was singing, *Lord, You Gave Me a Mountain*, he told his audience, "you're going nuts."

A little girl was brought up to the stage and Elvis gave her a sweet little kiss.

A fan gave him a crazy-coloured hat so he put it on and walked across the stage to the Sweet Inspirations. One of the Sweets took the hat and put it on.

Before giving out one scarf to a fan he wiped his chest on the inside of his jumpsuit with it.

Elvis sang every song beautifully but two songs really stood out. He said, "We have a new record out, ladies and gentlemen, and we'd like to sing it for you." He belted out *Hurt* once to a tremendous response and then he asked so cutely, "Wanna hear it again?" The crowd sure did, so El burst out with an even stronger version of *Hurt*. The second time around he made his voice go up really powerfully at the end. His one and only voice sure is a wonder to me!

Charlie Hodge brought a giant bulletin board that was covered with photos of Elvis up on stage to Elvis and El looked it over.

Without a doubt my favourite song was THE MAN's sincere version of *America the Beautiful*. To hear Elvis perform this intensely moving song (very moving because *ELVIS MADE IT VERY MOVING*) truly is a touching experience *no* fan should miss. This song alone, the way he performs the song, speaking part of it, the way he does, is enough to keep me in awe of the man for the rest of my life. I couldn't help but shed a few tears and during this song found myself saying silently, "God bless him and take care of him." Before that final song Elvis said, "I'd like to tell you something, you've been a fantastic audience. When was the last time we were here?" The audience yelled different numbers. Elvis asked, "Two years, three years? Three? Four years?" Then he said so amusingly, "Do I hear five? So—any time you want us back just give us a ring and we'll come back again." The loudest roar from the audience yet.

When his fans rushed the stage at the end of the show he tried to calm them down by saying, "Take it easy," and a shout of "Whoa-whoa-whoa." I was

about to go up to Elvis on the right side of the stage. There were no guards and not many people to the right of the stage which put me in a daze—I could get so close to Elvis with no guards to make me go back. But suddenly about 20 girls rushed at Elvis and a few of them got a hold of Elvis. Immediately a swarm of guards were carrying the girls away. Elvis just pulled himself away from the girls and smiled.

Being fortunate enough to experience Elvis up close, I got to know him as a person as well as a performer. As amazing and fantastic as he is, he really is just another human being like you and me. But a VERY, VERY SPECIAL human being that I have a VERY, VERY SPECIAL LOVE for. He was so nice and so friendly to his fans. He is such A NICE MAN! I LOVE HIM. Elvis—you're one humdinger of a singer and one humdinger of a NICE MAN!

WHO IS KING OF POP ?
by Vincent Preteroti

Being an Elvis fan for the last 20 years I have been bothered and annoyed by the non-Elvis fan, as I am sure many other Elvis fans have been. The non-fan takes every opportunity to put down the King. *Oops*, I slipped, let me reserve that title for that is what this article is all about.

The non-fan is always ready to give the crown to whatever or whoever may be the current trend. Candidates have been Pat Boone, Fabian, Little Richard, Chuck Berry, the Beatles, Bob Dylan, Elton John and many more. All or most have talent but to call them King of Rock is a joke. The non-fan always makes the same point that I am an Elvis fan and cannot give a fair opinion. So I took out my old record charts, from a leading national magazine, and analysed the charts for all to judge for themselves. I set up a points system and awarded points to every record to make the top 100, giving bonus points for every top 10 and number one record. The results are as follows:

1.	Elvis	1,812
2.	Beatles	935
3.	Pat Boone	802
4.	Ricky Nelson	732
5.	Connie Francis	695

The points awarded cover the years 1955 to 1974. The non-Elvis fan or the Beatle fan will say this is unfair because Elvis has been in the charts for a longer period of time. We will now look at the first seven years of each act.

ELVIS				BEATLES		
Year	Points	Total		Year	Points	Total
1956	*338	338		1964	374	374
1957	212	550		1965	174	548
1958	173	723		1966	80	628
1959	88	811		1967	105	733
1960	129	940		1968	67	800
1961	140	1080		1969	81	881
1962	105	1185		1970	54	935

*Now we must be fair to Elvis. In 1964 the Beatles cover 12 months for 374 points. Elvis came out later in 1956 so if we look at his first 12 months which we run into 1957 and Elvis comes up with 374 points which is a dead tie for Elvis and the Beatles for their first 12 months.

Now we will take a look at the Beatles near the end. Their chart popularity was dropping, no question. While this was happening Elvis was coming back into the charts. Let's look closer and compare the later years:

ELVIS				BEATLES		
Year	Points	Total		Year	Points	Total
1968	53	53		1968	67	67
1969	91	144		1969	81	148
1970	59	203		1970	54	202

Now you have it in black and white—that's the way it was. If you still have questions we'll take a quick look at the charts and I will try to answer them.

	Elvis	Beatles
1. Most 2-sided records	50	26
2. Most top 10 records	38	31
3. Most No. 1 records	20	18
4. Most weeks at No. 1	80	59

Compare No. 3 and 4 and Elvis is still Number One King.

I don't want to forget Elton John; for his first five years he has 503 points, so he will just have to wait before he has any hope of obtaining the Crown which Elvis and Elvis alone deserves. I would like to make one more comment on the total for Elvis (1,812) for this is the true meaning of the King. The rivals come and go and Elvis keeps right on going. A true test, for he survives the test of time. It is easy to make number one, for many artists make it, but it is hard to stay there and only Elvis has done that. It is always easy to look at the good years of an artist and say how great they are, but when we look at Elvis we see the high and low spots of the greatest star of all time and the one and only KING OF ROCK.

THE BUSINESS ON THE BUSINESS OF ELVIS PRESLEY

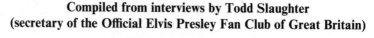

Compiled from interviews by Todd Slaughter
(secretary of the Official Elvis Presley Fan Club of Great Britain)

*Nicholas Parsons (TV personality, and star host of Anglia Television's *Sale of the Century*): I like all the great artistes—Ella, Frank, Sammy Davis, Lena, Pearl Bailey, Peggy Lee, Edith Piaf and Shirley Bassey. Elvis, though he's been going for over 20 years is still a "new boy" as far as the business is concerned, and I'm sure he'll join their ranks, if he isn't there already. He's a very talented artiste, swinging his hips, and making a strange melodic noise to tunes that have great feeling—he can't do anything wrong in my book.

*Yootha Joyce (Actress superb, and star of UK TV series *George and Mildred*): He's a real man, isn't he? I'd swap him for George any day. I especially like his rock 'n' roll material, but those smoothies do something to me, too. Elvis is King!

*Gary Newbon (Sports presenter for ATV, and sports writer for the *News of the World*): He's an outstanding performer who has stuck to his original talents. As a 10-year-old schoolboy at public school, I used to listen to Elvis' music on an illicit record player. *Teddy Bear, Don't, Jailhouse Rock, One Night, A Fool Such as I, Wooden Heart, Good Luck Charm* and *Crying in the Chapel*—they are my favourites, and I'd place *Blue Hawaii* as my favourite film. I only wish he'd work in Britain—soon I hope.

*Tony Prince (Radio Luxembourg DJ): Well, what can I say. All of Elvis' European fans know that I'm Elvis' number one fan. Having been to the States twice to see and record Elvis for Radio Luxembourg, I can only add to what I have said before, that it really is a mind-blowing experience.

*Cliff Richard (Worldwide superstar): Elvis was my idol from the beginning, and even today when I'm alone, I'll often put on the *King Creole* album. He's produced the most exciting pop music sounds of all time.

*Jimmy Savile, OBE (Radio and TV super-jock): Member number 11321 of the TTDC—Elvis will always be that to me. When I met him, when no one else was getting to meet the King, it was like meeting royalty. He is everything. He's a real star.

*Les Gray (Lead vocalist of "Mud"): We dropped Elvis material from our act, and we had put "him" back because we had so many requests. I too wish he would come to England, but he'll always be the "king" no matter what happens in the future.

*Alvin Stardust (Leading UK singer): No one can say Elvis hasn't arrived now, and he really is here to stay. I like all his oldies, yet it's a shame that many of his good LP tracks produced these days are forgotten. The *King Creole* album has to be my all time favourite.

*Gary Glitter: Elvis—he's still gotta be The King—even now. When he wiggled those hips in the old days the whole place would explode. Even I'm not as naughty as he was.

*Isaac Hayes (Academy Award-winning composer): There's got to be a valid reason why he's the most successful guy of the past decade. He's a giant, and any man who can influence all those people must have something. He's had expert guidance, of course, but there was a lot to guide.

*Guy Lombardo (Bandleader who's been watching them come and go for 48 years): Elvis is outstanding. He has great talent, handles himself beautifully, hasn't followed the dope route, has kept his head on his shoulders and is to be admired. No wonder he's the top attraction in America. Presley is here to stay.

*Dirk Bogarde (Top British actor): I am not exactly one of the in-crowd but I've long had a deep respect for Elvis Presley. I don't regard his movies as being classics of the screen, but I regard his personality and sheer sense of style as being outstanding. To be honest, I don't collect pop records as such—I'd much rather play classical or show albums for personal relaxation. But I find his records stimulating and—well—fun! He has a deep voice that is instantly recognisable and that is obviously the secret of his staying power. I'd say he has more versatility too, than the rest of the pop singers. He sings a ballad with warmth but when he really lets himself go on a rock 'n' roll number .... well, that is when he becomes truly exciting to hear. I doubt if I will ever work with Elvis Presley, but my admiration for his own kind of work is really boundless.

*Elton John: It was Scotty Moore's guitar riff when he was doing the *Steve Allan Show* that got me into rock music. I've been an Elvis fan since I was a kid.

*Mary Tyler Moore: I thought anyone who had been the centre of all that insanity for so long would have some of it rub off on him. But, after working in *Change of Habit* with him, I realised I'd never worked with a more gentlemanly, kinder man. He's gorgeous.

*Joe Cocker (Top rock singer): Elvis is the greatest Blues singer in the world today.

*John Lennon: Nothing really affected me until I heard Elvis. If there hadn't been an Elvis, there wouldn't have been the Beatles.

*Marty Wilde (Rock 'n' roll singer): Like every artiste to emerge during the rock scene Elvis was my influence and my idol.

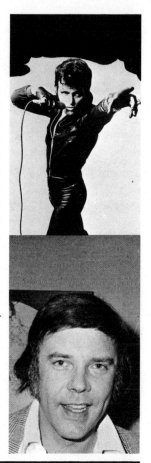

What if...

Our Epilogue by PAT McCARTHY

What would it have meant had Elvis not been discovered? Had he not walked into Sam Phillips' studio in Memphis in 1953, where would popular music be today? How would it have developed? Where would Elvis be today? The answer to these questions we'll never know, but just think about it for a moment, had Elvis not arrived, popular music may never have been grabbed by the neck and rocketed out of its mediocrity with such vigour and excitement as it was when *Heartbreak Hotel* and *Hound Dog* were the anthems of American youth.

Life might have been a little quieter across the US around the mid and late fifties had there not been a rock 'n' rollin' tornado named Presley sweeping from coast to coast leaving riots and controversy in his wake. Certainly record and guitar sales would not have had it so good.

What about Hollywood? His first movie, *Love Me Tender* had the dollars pouring in, it redeemed its production costs, over a million dollars, in its first three days of release. I'd say the studio bosses were glad he had been discovered.

What of his fans? What would they have done with their devotion, where would it have been channelled, or would it have remained dormant forever without the magic Presley touch to awaken it?

The US Army would not have had the extra complications they had to deal with when drafting US Private 53310761. Germany, and his European fans would have missed the excitement of having their "idol" if not within reach, at least on the same continent.

When he came marching home after his Army service Frank Sinatra would not have had his big night on coast to coast TV welcoming Elvis home, a show which ranks as one of the greatest all-time viewing ratings in US television history.

Years, and many more films and rfcords later the world would never have seen the dynamic reappearance of Elvis on TV, and Las Vegas, the scene of his return to splendour, would have missed its greatest tourist attraction in its history.

Think of the staggering amounts of money that have been generated due to Elvis, who has sold a fantastic 850 million dollars worth of records. His films have grossed more than 125 million dollars and countless millions have changed hands due to his

tours and personal appearances over the years. Think of all the artists that have acknowledged the influence of Elvis on their own careers; the list would fill a book itself.

But what of Elvis himself? What would have become of him had he not been in the right place at the right time, had he not been discovered, where would he be today? No one can tell!

Would he have become the electrician he was studying to be before his fame, or would he have stuck to truck driving to earn his living? Who knows!

Perhaps his Army service is the one event in his life that would have been the same, in that he would probably have been drafted the same time as he was. All the rest would have been different.

Would he have lived out his day to day life in Memphis? Probably! Passing "Graceland" regularly, maybe wondering who owned it. The answer to all these questions we can never know. What we do know is that Elvis "arrived" and besides his fame, fortune and glamour he has left us a legacy that money can't buy in terms of musical influence and most of all in bringing countless hours of happiness to millions of fans.

CROSSWORD ANSWERS